LOCHS

OF SCOTLAND

CONWAY
Bloomsbury Publishing Plc
50 Bedford Square, London, WC1B 3DP
29 Earlsfort Terrace, Dublin 2, Ireland

BLOOMSBURY, CONWAY and
the Conway logo are trademarks
of Bloomsbury Publishing Plc

First published in Great Britain 2022

Library of Congress Cataloguing-in-
Publication data has been applied for

ISBN: 978-1-4729-8293-3
ePub: 978-1-4729-8292-6
ePDF: 978-1-4729-8291-9

10 9 8 7 6 5 4 3 2 1

Typeset in FreightText Pro
Designed by Austin Taylor
Printed and bound in India by
Replika Press Pvt. Ltd.

MIX
Paper from
responsible sources
FSC® C016779

To find out more about our authors
and books visit www.bloomsbury.com
and sign up for our newsletters

Note: Reference to waters do not necessarily imply that access
and passage on those waters or their banks are legally permitted
or that they are safe in all conditions. The author and publishers
cannot be held responsible for any omissions of references to
hazards on these waters. Circumstances can change without
warning. The user should assess the situation using all
information available at the time and act appropriately.

LOCHS
OF SCOTLAND

The comprehensive guide to Scotland's most
fabulous inland and sea lochs

C❖NWAY

LONDON · OXFORD · NEW YORK · NEW DELHI · SYDNEY

40
41
39
42
38
37
35
36
34
30
33
32
29
31
27
28
26
43
25
20
24
19
18
45
23
21
17
22
16
46
47
48
15
14
50
49
13
6
12
9
5
7
4
3
11
8
10
2
1

CONTENTS

ACKNOWLEDGEMENTS

p.9   from *The Fleece* by John Dyer.

p.15   from *The Bonnie Banks o' Loch Lomond*, Anon.

p.24   from *The Old Soldier of Gareloch Head* by John Stuart Blackie.

p.28   from *The Bloody Sarks* by Ian Hall.

p.45   from *Inverary Epigram* by Robert Burns.

p.51   from *The Lord of the Isles* by Sir Walter Scott.

p.55   by John Marsden, reproduced by permission of Peter Burns, Birlinn Ltd.

p.67   from *Nora's Vow* by Sir Walter Scott.

p.72   from *The Lord of the Isles* by Sir Walter Scott.

p.79   from *The Stuarts of Appin* by James Hogg.

p.82   from *The Campbells are Coming* by Robert Burns.

p.90   from *Glen-na-h'Albyn*, Anon.

p.93   from *The Bothy in Glen Pean* by John Hargreaves.

p.97   from *The Stuarts of Appin* by James Hogg.

p.112   from *Sound the Pibroch* by Agnes Maxwell MacLeod.

p.116   from *The Bothy in Glen Pean* by John Hargreaves.

p.128   from *My Bonnie Moorhen*, Anon.

p.149   from *Loch Torridon* by Algernon Charles Swinburne.

p.152   from *Loch Maree Islands* by Kenneth C Mackenzie.

p.163   from *Beyond Allt-na-Harrie* by Joan Pittock Wesson.

p.166   from *A Man in Assynt* by Norman MacCaig.

p.170   from *Of My First Love* by Hugh MacDiarmid.

p.172   from *The Lord of the Isles* by Sir Walter Scott.

p.178   from *Henny Munroe* by Jim McLean.

p.183   Anon.

p.187   from *A Highland Glen near Loch Ericht* by Arthur Hugh Clough.

p.191   from *The Lord of the Isles* by Sir Walter Scott.

p.194   from *The Road to the Isles* by Kenneth MacLeod.

p.196   from *Loch Tay Boat Song* by Boulton & MacLeod.

p.200   from *The Lady of the Lake* by Sir Walter Scott.

p.202   from *The Lady of the Lake* by Sir Walter Scott.

Every effort has been made to trace authors. Bloomsbury are happy to correct any error or omission in future editions.

I wish to pay thanks to the following:
    Jim McLean, Brendan Paddy, Eddie Palmer and Helen Todd are among those who offered helpful information on many books.

    I have worked with Editorial Director Elizabeth Multon on several books. We each have a fair idea of how the others work even before we start, which results in a relaxed working relationship.

    This book would not have happened without the practical support of my wife, Becky, who sat at many a remote spot, waiting for me to appear in the distance. Also, to my sons Brendan and Ross, who tested the play value of many beaches at a time when junior school teachers agreed that they were learning more on what were, effectively, geography field trips than they would have done sitting in classrooms.

INTRODUCTION

Western Scotland has some of the best scenery in Europe, especially when looking at the lochs from the mountains or looking at the mountains from the lochs. Either can offer testing conditions where knowledge of safety on water or on the hills is essential, but this is just part of the challenge of getting maximum enjoyment from this superlative region.

This book introduces fifty of the infinite number of Scottish lochs and lochans, both tidal and inland. While sea lochs require tides to be taken into consideration and may be more exposed to the elements, inland lochs can also quickly produce testing conditions. Weather conditions can change fast and lochs are often remote. Winds can behave unpredictably as they find gaps between mountains and you may be a long way from anyone else, either on the water or on land. Even when there is road access, usage can be sparse and communications can be sporadic. Some trunk roads might see only a couple of cars an hour. At times self-reliance is essential. This is a region that is great for getting

The author collecting first-hand knowledge from the locals.

away from the crowds, and for finding peace and tranquillity as well as exquisite scenery.

The lochs in this book are mostly the larger ones, but not all of the big ones. Lochs have been omitted if they cannot be reached by public road, require ferries, or if they are not accessible from the water without going far from the coastline. Similarly, lochs that become so large that they are, effectively, open coastline have also been omitted. Others have been left out if the approach is over private estate roads, sometimes over very considerable distances, if portable craft need to be carried a long way to the water to launch or if commando tactics are needed to get afloat. If you enjoy the challenge of reaching the most inaccessible lochs and are prepared to obtain the permissions required, or meet the physical challenges of reaching the water, there are further lochs remaining to tempt you. The world's highest water on Everest has been paddled by kayak. All water in Scotland is easier to reach.

Some lochs are used for water storage or flood prevention and have been avoided as they often have shorelines in the form of broad bands of grey rock or boulders devoid of life. There is no shortage of more attractive lochs.

As well as stunning scenery, the lochs chosen have a wide variety of other interests, such as the history of clan warfare and Prince Charlie, urban aquatic playgrounds, military activity, warships, submarines, wildlife, ghost and monster reports, marinas, fish farms and fishing ports, serious rapids on rivers and at sea, castles, bridges, breweries and distilleries, transport routes from the challenging to pure fantasy, waterfalls, the Clearances, hydroelectric power, crannogs, powerboats, cruise ships and commandos. This immense variety shows up in unexpected places.

Get off the beaten track and discover what Scotland's lochs have to offer.

STUART FISHER

KEY

——————	River or canal
▬▬▬▬▬	Motorway
——————	Other road
▬▬▬▬▬	Railway
▭▭▭▭	Open water or sea
▭▭▭▭	Inter-tidal zone
▭▭▭▭	Built-up area
▭▭▭▭	Woodland

Scale 1:200,000
North is always at the top

COVID-19 NOTE

Please note that businesses have been subject to Covid-19 restrictions at the time of preparation of this book. Many have ceased to trade. Some will emerge again in old or new forms. Check on their status before visiting.

LOCH KEN

SMALL ISLANDS AND SMALL BOATS

Through Ken swift rolling down his rocky dale
JOHN DYER

LOCH KEN

The Water of Ken river rises as Polvaddoch Burn on Meikledodd Hill in the Southern Uplands, and flows southwards through Dumfries & Galloway to Loch Ken. Here it meets the River Dee and continues under this name to the Solway Firth.

The A762 runs alongside the water on the west side, while the A713 is further back from the east side.

Loch Ken is at its widest and most exposed at the northern end. However, an assortment of islands here shelter it from strong southerly winds that can cause large waves to arrive at this end of the loch. Shelter from the west comes in the form of the rounded bulk of Cairn Edward Hill, covered with the fir trees of Cairn Edward Forest, part of the Galloway Forest Park, and passed over in SR Crockett's *The Raiders*.

The width at the northern end suits

↓ Loch Ken viaduct crosses a narrow and shallow part of the loch.

↑ Galloway Activity Centre equipment at Ringbane.

↓ Cairn Edward Hill and Cairn Edward Forest.

sailing craft and windsurfers, operating from Lochside. Galloway Activity Centre at Parton offers a good range of activities on the water. Despite water skiers being able to use the loch from Ged Point to near the viaduct, water lilies still grow and survive from here to Glenlaggan and Loch Ken Marina, where powerboats operate and which is overlooked by a caravan site. A 16km/h speed limit applies south of this point.

The loch is crossed at its narrowest point by the Loch Ken viaduct, which used to carry the railway from Castle Douglas to Newton Stewart. Immediately after the viaduct the River Dee enters on the west side, opposite an assortment of tents and caravans, with kayaks in abundance.

The valley then widens out and the landscape becomes flatter and more cultivated. Islands make it difficult to pick the best line, but power lines across the loch are helpful in estimating distance along the loch. An isolated hillock near the shore at Parton is an old motte. Parton House also features in *The Raiders*.

Birdlife ranges from kingfishers and swans to pochard, greylag and Greenland white-fronted geese, for which the Ken-Dee Marshes are an RSPB reserve.

Crossmichael has a selection of boats, windsurfers and kayaks. The village also has a large white church with a round tower and spire midway along the side, but this is far less conspicuous than the small white church that stands alone in its graveyard at Bridgestone, on the far side of the loch. Another prominent structure is the fort wall at Crofts, with an archway that really stands out against the sky from the loch.

The loch steadily narrows until the barrage at Glenlochar where it is no wider than the River Dee, which flows away under the B795 bridge. Exit from the loch is not easy at the barrage. The premises of the electricity company is on the west side just before the barrage, slightly beyond a slipway leading down from a private house.

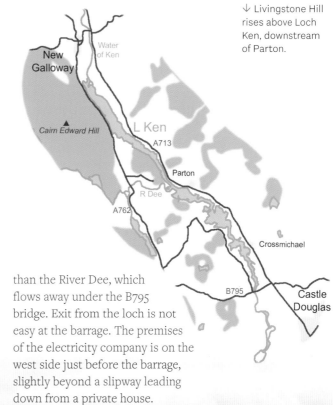

↓ Livingstone Hill rises above Loch Ken, downstream of Parton.

DISTANCE
14km from Parkrobbin to Glenlochar

OS 1:50,000 SHEETS
77 Dalmellington & New Galloway
83 Newton Stewart & Kirkcudbright

LOCH DOON

THE CASTLE SAVED FROM DROWNING

LOCH DOON

Along the east shore of Loch Doon is Dumfries and Galloway, as far as the Polnaskie Burn, otherwise the loch runs northwards across East Ayrshire. It is in the Galloway Forest Park as far as Black Craig on the east side and to the Garpel Burn on the west shore.

The approach from the north is along a single track road on the west side of the loch, surfaced until just south of Craigmalloch, where it turns west as an unsurfaced road used by timber lorries and popular with mountain bikers. Conifers in Carrick Forest are felled, but the pine trees seem to survive in a landscape where the mass of granite dictates the scenery.

Parking near the water is very limited. There are possibilities at Craigmalloch, where there are public toilets, and at the visitor centre at the northern end of the loch.

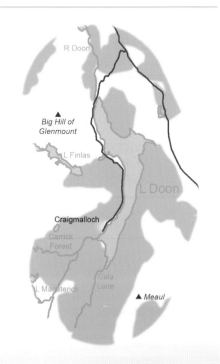

↓ Craiglee and part of Carrick Forest above Craigmalloch.

↓ Loch Doon Castle, rebuilt at Craigmalloch. Coran of Portmark and Meaul arise behind.

↑ Gala Lane feeds down into the loch at Loch Head.

Water is fed in at Loch Head by Gala Lane, seen falling steeply over rapids and under a bridge before reaching a peat bog area around the start of the loch, where some stone walls have been built.

Herons and cormorants can be seen, as well as smaller fliers, including wagtails and midges, and perhaps ospreys. A nature reserve has golden eagles, peregrine falcons and black-throated divers.

Carrick Lane adds water from Loch Macaterick and Loch Riecawr.

Scottish lion and Saltire flags on Castle Island at Craigmalloch mark the remains of the 13th century Doon Castle, which resisted a siege by the English in 1335. Although small, the castle has been noted for the quality of its masonry, more typical of major castles. When the loch water level was raised by 8.2m in the 1930s for hydroelectric power, the castle was dismantled and rebuilt on the west shore, overlooking a point with

↓ Castle Island with the remains of the castle and Black Craig behind.

↑ Loch Doon Dam at the end of the loch was built in 1937.

small sandy beaches and one of several red lifebelts that have been positioned conspicuously down the loch.

Raising the water level drowned a number of surrounding islands that would have otherwise added picturesque views to the loch.

The southern end of the loch is dominated by hills, with 695m Meaul, 623m Coran of Portmark and 528m Black Craig on the east side and 523m Craiglee to the west, after which the land drops away to be flatter at the northern end of the loch.

Most of the boats on the loch belong to anglers and are moored near Lambdoughty Farm.

The Garpel Burn brings in water from Derclach Loch and Loch Finlas, opposite the Polnaskie Burn which delivers Loch Muck's contribution.

The lower topography at the north

end features 330m Muckle Eriff Hill and 382m Big Hill of Glenmount, with a conspicuous caravan site above the loch.

Loch Doon Dam was designed by Sir Alexander Gibb & Partners and completed in 1937 by Sir Alfred McAlpine & Sons. The road runs across the top of the slightly curved 300m structure, of which the centre section is a mass concrete gravity structure. The fish pass is a spiral inside a circular concrete tower. The dam stores water for the upper three power stations on the River Dee. Water not taken leaves as the River Doon in Ness Glen.

DISTANCE_____

9km from Loch Head to Loch Doon Dam.

OS 1:50,000 SHEET_____

77 Dalmellington & New Galloway

LOCH LOMOND

THE QUEEN OF SCOTTISH LOCHS

O ye'll tak' the high road, and I'll tak' the low road,
And I'll be in Scotland a'fore ye,
But me and my true love will never meet again,
On the bonnie, bonnie banks o' Loch Lomond.
ANON

LOCH LOMOND

Cut by Ice Age glaciation, Loch Lomond is up to 190m deep and was formerly a sea loch, despite its surface now being 7m above sea level.

It was once known for waves without wind, fish without fins and a floating island. There are still waves without wind as the weather changes at short notice and waves rise quickly, leaving swells in calms after storms. Visitors need to be ready to protect themselves if conditions do deteriorate. Winds may seem unpredictable as they find gaps between the adjacent mountains.

The fish without fins were vipers swimming between the islands, but there are trout, salmon and powan, a form of freshwater herring. The loch has also produced a 21.6kg pike.

Defoe was dubious about the floating islands in his book *A Tour Through the Whole Island of Great Britain* and about the claim that the loch water turned wood to stone.

↓ The ferry waits at Ardlui.

↑ The A82 now runs on piers at Pulpit Rock.

↓ Ben Vorlich stands above Ardlui.

for the continuous distant noise of traffic on the A82 and the much more intrusive noise of motorbikes. At the southern end the loch opens out and the water becomes shallower and much busier, this being Glasgow's aquatic playground with power boats, jet skis, water skiers, sailing dinghies, angling boats, canoeists, paddleboarders and more.

Running southwards down the Loch Lomond & the Trossachs National Park, which was set up in 2002, the loch is fed by the River Falloch, which was canalized below Inverarnan in 1844.

Launching at the northern end is not easy, although Ardlui Marina, tucked in behind the Ardlui Hotel and a group of chalets, are helpful and offer wake boarding and other sports. Some lay-bys can be used for portable craft.

In summer a passenger ferry crosses

Boats have used the loch since prehistoric times. The 18m paddle steamer *Marion* plied its trade on the loch from 1818.

Effectively, it is two lochs. The northern end is narrow and quiet, except

the loch from Ardlui to the West Highland Way, Scotland's first and most popular long-distance footpath, which follows the east side of the loch to Balmaha. It winds through oak, conifer and birch woods with bracken and outcrops of weathered rock facing on to gravel beaches. The wildest and most scenic section of the loch shore is from the head of the loch down to Rowardennan.

The west side has deciduous trees including ash, rowan, hazel and beech, plus spruce, pine and larch. Winding through these is the railway line from Fort William to Glasgow, above the narrow and twisting A82 that follows the shoreline. At Pulpit Rock the road began to subside into the loch and has had to be rebuilt on piers.

A spit runs out from Rubha Ban, pushing craft over towards Island I Vow which is planted with daffodils, perhaps by the monks of a former monastery here. There are also castle remains.

The east bank becomes part of the

↓ Penstocks feed down from Loch Sloy. Beyond are Beinn Narnain and Beinn Ime.

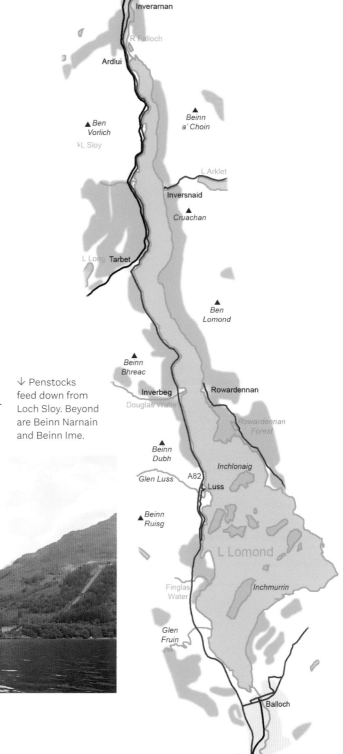

Stirling council area as the boundary drops down from 770m Beinn a' Choin. To the west is 985m Ben Vorlich. A nature reserve has red and roe deer, Scottish wildcats, feral goats, golden eagles, buzzards, black grouse, tree pipits, wood warblers, redstarts and spotted and pied flycatchers, which have yet to make progress against the midges.

Sroin Uaidh has Rob Roy's Cave, which was also used by Robert the Bruce.

Until the Ice Age, Inveruglas Water would have flowed from Loch Sloy via

↑ Tarbet with Ben Donich and the Cobbler beyond.

Loch Arklet to Loch Katrine. Penstocks feed water down to the power station. The dam on Loch Sloy was the first project of the North of Scotland Hydro Electric Board in 1946. Prisoners of war were used as part of the labour force. The water level of Loch Sloy is 150m above that of Loch Lomond, which receives water from both directions out of hanging valleys.

A passenger ferry crosses from the power station to Inversnaid, passing the castle site on Inveruglas isle. Inversnaid

is recalled by Gerard Manley Hopkins' *Inversnaid* and Wordsworth's poem *To a Highland Girl*. Angus Downie's *The Heart of Scotland by Waterway* describes canoeing from Balloch to here and then moving across to Loch Katrine in the days when stage coaches were still being used for transport.

Ben Vane at 916m and A'Chrois at 848m are clear as they stand well back from the west side of Loch Lomond, unlike 536m Cruachan, which crowds the east side. A settlement of chalets finds space by the road on the west side of the loch at Inveruglas.

The railway leaves at Tarbet, using a dry gap to reach Loch Long. This gap is more than 2km long, but in 1263 King Magnus of Mann had his ships dragged through in order to use them to pillage the Lennox lands around Loch Lomond.

Above Rob Roy's Prison sits 974m Ben Lomond of mica schists. The name comes perhaps from the Old British *llumon*, beacon. It is known to have been climbed in 1758 and the first record of cutting ice steps was here in 1812. The view from the top is said to be the best in the southern Highlands.

Rubha Mór, with its Old Military Road on the far side of the A82, lies between 681m Beinn Bhreac and 597m Beinn Uird. Rowardennan is the roadhead on the east side of the loch. From here there is a passenger ferry in summer across to Inverbeg where the Douglas Water discharges out into the loch past the Inverbeg Gallery and a holiday park of chalet accommodation.

Opposite 642m Beinn Dubh is Ross Point, beyond which Camas an Losgainn begins to open up the width of Loch Lomond at the foot of Rowardennan Forest. The hills begin to drop away and the loch becomes studded with islands.

Luss has the accolade of the prettiest village in Scotland. It was Glendarroch in Scottish Televion's *Take the High Road* soap opera (later named *High Road*). Prominent is St Kessog's church, which was built by Sir James Colquhoun in 1875. It has a tenth-century sarcophagus with medieval effigy of St Kessog and coffins that may be sixth century. Further attractions include the Clan Colquhoun Heritage & Luss Visitor Centre and the Thistle Bagpipe Works.

It was said that there were 60 islands in Loch Lomond, with 60 crags occupied by 60 eagles' nests, with the eagles foretelling major events by screaming. Geoffrey of Monmouth's *Historia Regum Britanniae* claims King Arthur killed the Picts and Scots taking refuge from him on the islands. A more common claim is that there are 22 islands, although up to

49 including significant islets. There are names for 38. Some are inhabited, calling for the services of a sailing postman.

Inchlonaig was planted with yews for bows by Robert the Bruce. The Colquhoun chief and Rob Roy met here to agree blackmail arrangements. Inchconnachan, Colquhoun's island, has wallabies. Mallards and wagtails are more common residents on the route from Fraoch Eilean past a wall of rhododendrons. A statue of Wee Peter

↑ Holiday chalets at Inverbeg below Doune Hill.

↓ Ben Lomond gives its name to the loch.

↓ Oaks and bracken by a beach on the east side of the loch.

↑ Luss, said to be the prettiest village in Scotland.

→ Wee Peter stands in Bandry Bay.

has stood on a column in the middle of Bandry Bay since 1890, an item left over from a London building project.

Nestled below 595m Beinn Ruisg, Inchtavannach, or monk's island, used to have a monastery. Less peaceful these days, its south-east coast is a base for seaplane sightseeing flights over the loch.

To the south-west of Inchmoan is the small Inchgalbraith. Rossdhu House, with a tower and chapel on its north-west side and now a golf course to the south, was the seat of the Colquhouns and was visited by Johnson and Boswell in 1773. Johnson went out in a boat, even though he disliked the islands and their lack of lawns. He records in *A Journey to the Western Islands of Scotland* landing on Inchlonaig and Inchgalbraith, where ospreys nested every year on the castle.

Off Ross Park and the entrance to Finglas Water across to the Loch Lomond national nature reserve, the loch is at its widest at 7km.

Inchmurrin is the largest and southernmost of the islands. It is named after St Mirrin, who founded an early Christian church on the islands. There are ruins of a Lennox castle in the south-west corner.

Continuing the line from Inchmurrin are Creinch, Torrinch, Inchcailloch all on the Highland Boundary Fault. This is where the Highlands give way

← Rossdhu House, seat of the Colquhouns.

to the Lowlands. People south of here are sassenachs or lowlanders but not necessarily English.

Boturich Castle guards the east side of the loch as it narrows down. Next to it is Balloch Castle, the seat of Lennox power. The existing castle was built in 1808, for a banker. It is surrounded by an 81ha country park with Victorian walled gardens and unusual stained glass. A moat at the end, with towpath, has the River Leven carry water away towards the Clyde.

The west side of the loch is Cameron country, the name appearing frequently, not least for Cameron House, rebuilt in 1865 after a fire.

Rocks and gravels in glacier moraine deposits formed a dam 8m above sea level. Antiquities include a cairn and chambered cairn. Modern attractions include a pair of popular slipways, a cruise pier, National Park Gateway Centre, Sea Life Loch Lomond Aquarium, Loch Lomond Shores mall, theatre, shops and six-storey Drumkinnon Tower, a world away from the Ardlui end of the loch.

↓ *The Maid of the Loch* at Balloch.

DISTANCE
34km from Ardlui to Balloch

OS 1:50,000 SHEET
56 L Lomond & Inveraray

Loch Lomond and Trossachs National Park advice

SAFETY

A lot of effort goes into teaching responsible outdoor activities. Large lochs, particularly Loch Lomond, can be subject to sudden changes in the weather. People are advised to watch for these and to get off the water before conditions deteriorate significantly, and find or erect shelter. Conditions can quickly reach the point where it is no longer safe to go across to the sheltered side of the loch, if there is one.

People are also advised to watch for the first signs of hypothermia, which can happen even on a relatively mild day, again getting off the water and getting shelter as soon as possible. If one of a group is showing symptoms, others are likely to follow, with steadily deteriorating prospects.

CAMPING

One of the valuable aspects of the Land Reform (Scotland) Act of 2003 was to allow wild camping, subject to certain common-sense restrictions. It has been a right that has attracted many outdoor enthusiasts to the wilds of Scotland. However, in 2017 the Loch Lomond & Trossachs National Park Authority brought in by-laws that make wild camping illegal across a great swathe of the southern Highlands between March and September. The authority says that only 4% of the national park is affected, but that is nearly all waterside. Take out the mountains and the figure suddenly looks very large. Take out the physically impossible locations, such as lochs and banks of boulders leading up to trunk roads and we are talking about the majority. For mountaineers, camping is likely to be permitted higher up in more exposed locations, not ideal for those affected by the weather and needing to shelter.

The new requirement is to use formal campsites. Officials will not take action in what they consider to be genuine emergencies, normally if campsites have been booked in advance and park authorities telephoned to advise of changes, although there may not be telephone availability. Many will not book campsites in advance because they expect to go home at the end of the day or at least get clear of the national park. Less experienced users will take chances with the conditions rather than risk £500 fines and criminal records.

In 2017–2020, 2,492 campers (3.5%) had their details taken and there are concerns these are being held longer than permitted by privacy laws. In that period seven campers received criminal records, none solely for camping. Findings suggest that 'incidences of specific camping-related antisocial behaviour have remained low', although locals are pleased that activities such as tree felling and car burning by others have ceased.

Campers will be required to bring their own firewood, nonsense for most paddlers, hikers, climbers and cyclists.

A further ban is on sleeping in vehicles. We are regularly told not to drive when tired but to stop and rest, at which point one may fall

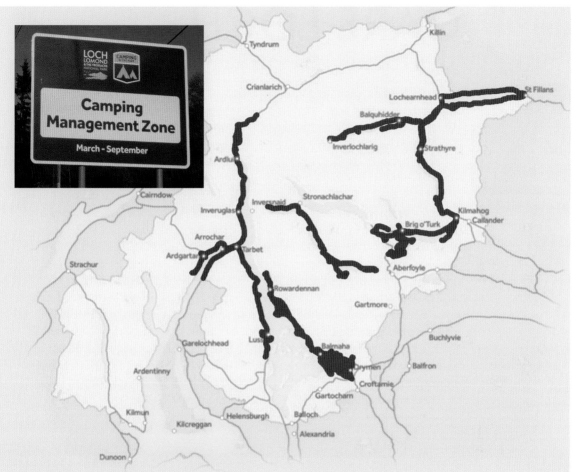

asleep, much preferable to doing so at the wheel. A typical scenario might be someone returning after an active weekend on the water or hills on the west coast and now relaxed after coming in out of the weather, comfortable after a meal. There is a continuous banned sleep area from south of Crianlarich to south of Luss, over 30km, before reaching the approach to Glasgow and the motorway network. The restriction is little shorter between St Fillans and Callander on the east side of the park.

The park authority cannot prevent drivers from stopping in public lay-bys but if you are tired you don't want to try to rest with traffic speeding past a couple of metres away and you don't want to be making decisions about whether a lay-by belongs to the highway authority or the park, which could make a huge difference to the way you might be treated.

The Scottish Countryside Rangers Association, Scottish Sports Association, Royal Yachting Association Scotland, Scottish Canoe Association, Ramblers Scotland and Mountaineering Scotland have all expressed concern about these by-laws.

04 GARE LOCH

BASE FOR NUCLEAR SUBMARINES

GARE LOCH

And here we often met,
When with lightsome foot we sped,
O'er the green and grassy knolls
At the Gareloch Head.
JOHN STUART BLACKIE

Gare Loch cuts south-east to join the Firth of Clyde. It is synonymous with the Faslane naval base and movements are restricted for security reasons. It all forms part of the Clyde Dockyard Port of Gareloch & Loch Long and is deemed to be a Narrow Channel for the purposes of the International Regulations for Preventing Collisions at Sea with various rules, including restrictions on the use of whistles.

There are additional restrictions when nuclear submarines are being moved

↓ The Faslane facilities, ending with a floating drydock. The Strone rises to Beinn a' Mhanaich and a further ridge to Beinn Tharsuinn.

and they frequently exercise surfaced or submerged in Gare Loch. Three vertical green lights and pennant 9 give warning of ship movements that may last an hour, when the area has to be cleared by other boats. Restrictions are imposed by Ministry of Defence police in fast RIBs. Iain Banks' novel *Complicity* describes them doing so as a Vanguard submarine arrives at Faslane.

The head of Gare Loch is only 1km from Loch Long and Loch Goil, but the intervening ridge is some 200m high.

Streams are imperceptible, except at the Rhu Narrows near the southern end of the loch. The head of the loch drains, leaving an area of sharp stones, mussels and barnacles. The Route 81 Youth Project slip is located at the head of the

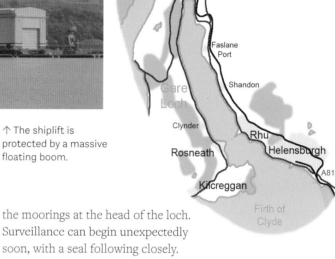

loch, but most people with portable boats need to launch from one of the roads that follow the shore closely except at the naval base. A high seawall needs to be negotiated, but there are steps down.

Amenities in Garelochhead include a play area, football pitches and toilets. A cuckoo calls from the surrounding woods in the spring and oystercatchers frequent the shore. A church with a spire breaks the roofline and there is an old ornamental iron drinking fountain.

Sailing and windsurfing take place past

↑ The shiplift is protected by a massive floating boom.

the moorings at the head of the loch. Surveillance can begin unexpectedly soon, with a seal following closely.

The Clyde submarine base occupies the facilities used by the Home Fleet at the end of the Second World War, starting at Rowmore. Submarines bottom off Rowmore Point.

Protected by a massive floating boom is the shiplift. This structure with its reinforced concrete deck resting on 822 tubular piles 50m long is at the heart of the maintenance facility for the submarine fleet. Added in 2009 was a 200m-long floating jetty built in nearby Greenock.

Faslane Bay is a Protected & Restricted Area with extensive regulations rigidly enforced. When shipping movements are taking place it may be permissible for small boats to use the edge of the loch outside the line of black and yellow barges moored down the west side.

Opposite the main gate of the base is

↑ Garelochhead Forest on the ridge above Clynder.

a chapel site and a peace camp.

A patch of woodland containing a motte on the east side comes at the return of the east shore to civilian rule. Shandon boasts the Shandon School of Equitation, including an indoor school, but boaters will be more interested in Blairvadach Outdoor Education Centre with its sailing courses.

The rounded ridge on the west side is partly planted with Garelochhead Forest and has been taken over to an extent by a colourful display of yellow gorse. Behind the low seawall at Clynder are a picnic area and toilets.

Stroul Bay is used by seaplanes and has moorings below a hilltop aerial, giving way to a substantial works constructed on Limekiln Point at Rosneath.

The Royal Northern & Clyde Yacht Club, Scotland's oldest, was founded in 1824 and has a listed clubhouse and a jetty at Rhu, named after the Gaelic for promontory. It precedes the spit causing the Rhu Narrows where tidal velocities can run to 9km/h (5 knots). The spit, terminated by Rhu Point light beacon, helps restrict approach to the loch for naval defence purposes. Closure of Rhu Narrows is indicated by a red over two green lights or a red flag with a white diagonal.

Beyond the seawall is Rhu and Shandon Church with a flat-roofed tower and eight small spires. The churchyard has a statue to engineer Henry Bell.

Rosneath Bay is backed by a forest walk and West Scotland Caravan Park, and ends with Castle Point Light. It faces across to Rhu Marina, the inshore rescue boat station, Royal Corps of Transport jetty, landing craft and wreck. Canmore was a wartime seaplane base. Now eider ducks nest on the pontoons.

The more refined air of Helensburgh begins to emerge at Glenarn Gardens, a woodland garden with a burn, daffodils, primulas, bluebells, rhododendrons, magnolias and embothriums. Kidston Park at Cairndhu Point, dating from the late 19th century, has a bandstand, play equipment, toilets and picnic benches.

DISTANCE
10km from Garelochhead to Helensburgh

OS 1:50,000 SHEETS
56 L Lomond & Inveraray
63 Firth of Clyde

TIDAL CONSTANTS
Garelochhead: Dover +0120
Shandon: Dover +0110
Rhu Pier: Dover +0110
Helensburgh: Dover +0120

SEA AREA
Malin

RESCUE
Inshore lifeboat: Helensburgh
All weather lifeboat: Troon

It also has a large car park, which avoids later problems with parking restrictions on the A814.

This was found the most convenient place to run two submarine cables across the loch. The beach is of stones, mussels and barnacles. The view across the River Clyde towards Greenock, past a large green dolphin marking the channel, is panoramic.

Ardencaple Castle was built to the north-west of Helensburgh. On the north side of the town is the Hill House of 1903, considered to be Charles Rennie Mackintosh's finest domestic architecture. Original and idiosyncratic, it was designed for publisher Walter Blackie as a family residence. It has a harled exterior and makes comprehensive use of coloured glass in the interior. Mackintosh also designed the furniture and the building now contains a display about him.

↑ The Rhu Point Light Beacon stands only 200m from the south-west side of the loch.

↓ Kidston Park, the most westerly end of Helensburgh, under an autumn sunrise.

LOCH LONG

STRAIGHT ENOUGH FOR A TORPEDO RANGE

LOCH LONG

The Campbell and the Cameron, MacDonald o' Glencoe
Ranked alang wi' Gregorach and marched o'er the snow
Far o'er the loch frae Arklet Glen and doon the past Parlan
By Loch Long whose shores are held by the thieves o' MacFarlane.
IAN HALL

There are lochs longer than Loch Long, but few are straighter. It is almost possible to travel the 20km from Succoth to Ardentinny in a straight line, as a result of glaciation.

At its head Loch Long is fed by Loin Water, which rises at the foot of Ben Vane and flows into the loch by the A83 bridge. There is parking on the abandoned section of road on the south-west side of the bridge.

Loch Long is a sea loch, heading south-west through Argyll & Bute to the Firth of Clyde. This orientation funnels the prevailing headwind, with the loch subject to squalls. Tidal flows outwards begin 1h 20min after Dover high water and inwards from 4h 40min before Dover high water, increasing to 2km/h (1 knot) at the mouth.

↓ Beinn Narnain and A' Chrois, which are two of the Arrochar Alps.

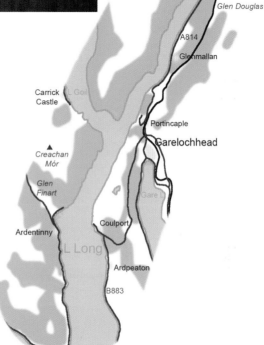

← The former Admiralty Torpedo Testing Station.

The loch forms part of the Clyde Dockyard Port of Gareloch and Loch Long and is considered to be a Narrow Channel as defined by the Collision Regulations. No craft is allowed within 150m of naval areas. Submarines exercise on the surface and submerged. Upper Loch Long used to be a torpedo range with targets, buoys, submarine cables and beacons at regular intervals down both sides of the loch until the end of the range 1km before Cnap Point.

The western bank is the Cowal Peninsula. Ardgartan Forest forms part

DISTANCE
23km from Succoth to Gairletter

OS 1:50,000 SHEET
56 Loch Lomond & Inveraray

TIDAL CONSTANTS
Arrochar: Dover +0110
Lochgoilhead: Dover +0110
Coulport: Dover +0110

SEA AREA
Malin

RESCUE
Inshore lifeboat: Helensburgh
All weather lifeboat: Troon

of the Argyll Forest Park, which surrounds the head of the loch and takes in most of the west bank. It features moorland, conifer plantations and surviving oakwood, plus Argyll's Bowling Green.

Arrochar, one of the places the fictional captain Para Handy called home, is where his crew had a particularly

↑ Arrochar, overlooked by Cruach Tairbeirt, the dry valley, Ben Reoch and Tullich Hill, from Loin Water mouth.

↓ The Glenmallan ammunition jetty.

bad attack of midges. The village is surrounded by the diorite Arrochar Alps. Peaks making up this range include Beinn Narnain, 926m high, and the 884m Cobbler, named from the shape of its summit, which has lots of bare rock to keep climbers occupied. Between the Arrochar Alps there is a 2km dry valley running eastwards to Tarbet on Loch Lomond. This gap is used by the A83 and the Crianlarich to Glasgow railway, which continues down the east bank to Portincaple.

In 1771 it was surveyed by James Watt as a potential canal route.

The former Admiralty Torpedo Testing Station on the western side of the loch, beside the old military road, which is now the A83, stands burnt out after a fire in 2007. It was an early reinforced concrete jetty from 1915. Public access is not allowed.

Swallows and gannets hunt above the water, the latter looking down through the clear depths on to cod, congers, dabs, flounders, mackerel, plaice and rays. The rocks are covered with barnacles, mussels and assorted wracks, while deciduous trees screen the banks.

Forest Holidays' chalets are located at Ardgartan on the alluvium brought down by Croe Water. The A83 then follows Glen Croe to the Rest & Be Thankful Pass, subject to repeated landslips.

Glen Mallan jetty has a 150m prohibited area, served by ammunition ships supplying the DM Glen Douglas munitions depot. These ships accelerate quickly and throw up metre-high washes that can break heavily.

Both shores rise steeply as far as Cnap Point, which is marked by a prominent white cone with orange stripes. The mountains gradually decline in height but are close to shore. Beinn Reithe at 655m, for example, has its peak only 1.7km from the water.

The A814 moves away at the Finnart Ocean Terminal, leaving 8km with no lochside roads. The oil terminal has three piers for tankers up to 300,000 tonnes.

At the terminal's centre is a traditional stone house with pipelines crossing the lawns and passing the windows.

Opposite Portincaple is Meall Daraich and the Carraig nan Ròn light column on which an oystercatcher has been found nesting. The column marks the north-eastern side of the end of Loch Goil.

Power lines cross high above Loch Long at a point just 1.5km from the head of Gare Loch, so close that the two lochs almost cross.

A massive structure at Port an Lochain is the RNAD Coulport Trident submarine Explosive Handling Jetty. It is 200m x 80m x 47m high and is moored in more than 80m of water after being towed up the Clyde. It was the world's biggest floating concrete dock at 85,000 tonnes. Technically, it is extremely advanced, having compensation for the rolling motion of a ship and responding to tidal

↓ Discharging at the Finnart Ocean Oil Terminal.

rise and fall and is able to remove and replace nuclear reactors safely. It has been designed to withstand 300km/h winds, 0.2g earthquake forces and collision by 100,000-tonne tankers bound for the Finnart Ocean Terminal.

The facility is not visible from inland and protected by line after line of security fencing, vast amounts of razor wire and batteries of video cameras and watchtowers. This makes the waterside rather tame by comparison, with an exclusion zone and a restricted area that keeps other craft to the west side of the loch. Security is ensured by police launches staffed by extremely polite policemen whose job would be easier if markers of some kind or leading lines were to be placed at the requisite distance offshore to offer guidance on the location of the edge of the restricted area. Three vertical green lights and pennant 9 give warning of ship movements when the area has to be cleared by other boats. When nuclear submarines are present the approach becomes less polite. Robin Lloyd-Jones was chased by marines with submachine guns in an inflatable after he paddled too close to one, described in his kayaking book *Argonauts of the Western Isles*.

Between Shepherd's Point beacon and Ravenrock Point light structure is Finart Bay at the end of Glen Finart. All grey squirrels in this part of the country are descended from a pair released here in 1890. The Ardentinny hotel at Dunoon has been a prominent landmark since the early 1700s.

On the east shore a measured distance may be marked for vessels wishing to conduct speed measurements.

The lochside roads now begin again, Coulport being sited at the end of the B883. The Firth of Clyde lies ahead with Cloch Point opposite and the houses of Gourock stacked up, but this does not mean a return to mass civilization. Mink are reported to live among the shoreline rocks at Ardpeaton.

A possible landing is at Gairletter Point where there is Gairletter Caravan Park and the inlet to a boathouse beside the road.

LOCH GOIL

SHARED BY YACHTS AND NUCLEAR SUBMARINES

06

Rising on Ben Donich as the Allt Glinne Mhóir, water flows south across Argyll & Bute, becoming the River Goil. Tides reach the stone rapids below the B839 bridge at Lochgoilhead, from where the river quickly opens out to form Loch Goil, the head of which drains. The tidal flow is imperceptible.

The village of Lochgoilhead is Victorian, but many wooden holiday chalets and caravans in the Drimsynie Estate Holiday Village on the west side of the head of the loch are modern. On the mountainside above them is a cave. There are lots of activities for visitors: boating, waterskiing, subaqua, sea angling, pony trekking, climbing and forest walks. The European Sheep & Wool Centre is located with shearing and

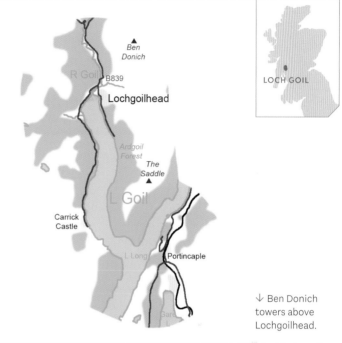

LOCH GOIL

↓ Ben Donich towers above Lochgoilhead.

↑ Looking up the loch past
Cruach nam Miseag.

↓ Superior lochside
tree house.

sheepdog demonstrations.

The loch is largely surrounded by Ardgoil Forest, mostly part of the 210 sq km Argyll Forest Park, itself part of the Loch Lomond & the Trossachs National Park, and projects into the Cowal peninsula.

Loch Goil is like a fjord, on the east side contained by the Steeple at 390m, 389m Tom nan Gamhna, 502m Càrn Glas, from which waterfalls descend, 655m Beinn Reithe, the Saddle at 521m, 370m Tom Molach and 441m Clach Bheinn. The west side meanwhile has 606m Cruach nam Miseag, 661m Sgurr a' Choinnich and 400m Cruach an Draghair as some of the salient points.

A catholic assortment of birds might be seen: swans, mallards, curlews, oystercatchers, common and black-backed gulls, wagtails, herons, cormorants and eider ducks, with eagles circling above. Assorted wracks give a brown shoreline to contrast with the green of the trees in the summer. The Lettermay Burn joins in one of the few areas not forested.

All the holiday activity belies the fact that this is part of the Clyde Dockyard Ports and is a Narrow Channel for navigation. The Douglas Pier is the base for noise testing at the Admiralty Trials Range, with a number of rafts down the east side of the loch and there may be buoys joined by wire. The range is used by nuclear submarines, especially during the day on weekdays, as shown by red flags on Douglas and Carrick Castle piers. Small craft may be able to pass on the west side of the loch.

Houses around the Lodge have

← Carrick Castle at the foot of Cruach a' Bhuic.

everything from decking to the ultimate in tree houses. From between the rhododendrons cloaking the bank a number of ropes and cables slip surreptitiously into the water, apparently heading for the range. Those bushes form an unlikely backdrop for rocks used by seals.

From Rubha na Beithe on the east side the loch is edged by low grey cliffs with trees right to the brink.

The prominent 14th-century Carrick Castle is on a rock with views both up the loch and to its mouth and shows the development from hall house to tower house. In 1651 it was fortified in case it

↑ Seals and rhododendrons.

↓ Rubha Ardnahein's flat green grass contrasts with the rest of the forested scenery around the loch.

was besieged by Commonwealth troops. John Campbell of Carrick, the then owner, was suspected of being in league with the 9th Earl of Argyll as a supporter of Montrose. The castle was taken by the Marquess of Atholl and lost its roof in 1685. Eventually, it fell into ruin but is currently being restored.

Rubha Ardnahein, which appears as an incongruous bright green meadow, has a steel frame light with a dayglo panel, not enough to have prevented a wreck in Toll nam Muc. A ship mooring buoy and large navigation buoys show that large craft are expected in this area.

Above Rubha nan Eoin is a tall pylon supporting power lines across Loch Long, which is met here. Backed by bracken at the foot of 144m Meall Daraich is the islet of Carraig nan Ròn or Seal Rock, which has a white cylindrical light column.

DISTANCE
10km from Lochgoilhead to Portincaple

OS 1:50,000 SHEET
56 Loch Lomond & Inveraray

TIDAL CONSTANTS
Lochgoilhead: HW Dover +0120, LW Dover +0030
Coulport: Dover +0110

SEA AREA
Malin

RESCUE
Inshore lifeboat: Luss
All weather lifeboat: Troon

Opposite is a dip in the cliffs, lining up with the head of the Gare Loch, and it may be that Loch Goil continued in this direction in earlier times before being intercepted by glacial action in Loch Long.

→ Contorted rock folding on the east side of the loch.

LOCH ECK

BEWARE OF LITTLE PEOPLE

07

Running mostly due south in Argyll & Bute, the narrow Loch Eck bisects the Argyll Forest Park at the heart of the Cowal peninsula. Indeed, Loch Eck Forest is on both sides, mostly firs used for forestry.

The A815 runs along the east shore and it is possible to launch from various lay-bys, although these are not easy to identify from the water. Better are some of the picnic areas, particularly the one at Dornoch Point, where it is possible to pull off the road. There are picnic tables and benches and an attractive stand of pines, with larches, hazels and bracken adding more variety and alders further down the loch.

The peaty River Cur meanders into the head of the loch past marshy reed beds, having passed less than 2km from Loch

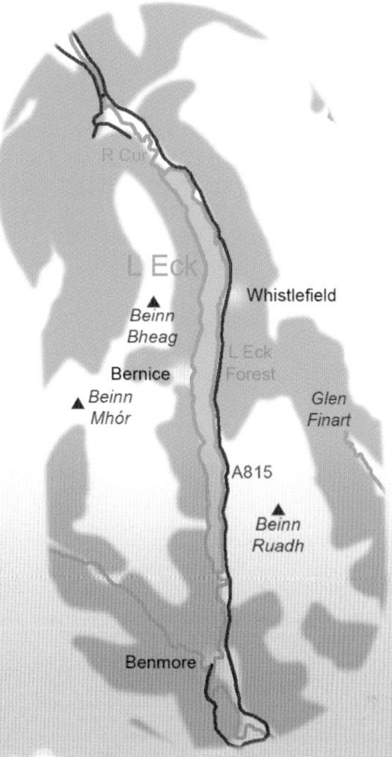

LOCH ECK

R Cur

L Eck

Whistlefield

Beinn
Bheag

L Eck
Forest

Bernice

Glen
Finart

▲ Beinn
Mhór

A815

Beinn
Ruadh

Benmore

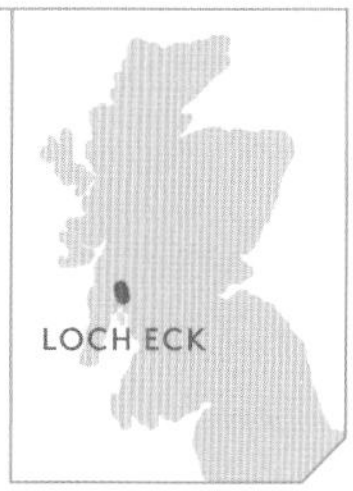

↓ Beinn Dubhain
above the head
of the loch.

↑ One of the tree-lined beaches at Dornoch Point.

↓ A stand of pines at Whistlefield.

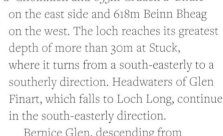

Fyne. Cormorants and swans live here, as does the powan, a freshwater herring that exists only here and in Loch Lomond.

The sides of the loch climb away steeply to 649m Beinn Dubhain, 661m Sgurr a' Choinnich and 635m Cruach a' Bhuic

on the east side and 618m Beinn Bheag on the west. The loch reaches its greatest depth of more than 30m at Stuck, where it turns from a south-easterly to a southerly direction. Headwaters of Glen Finart, which falls to Loch Long, continue in the south-easterly direction.

Bernice Glen, descending from before 741m Beinn Mhór, provides a wind gap from which the wind can spill out both ways onto Loch Eck, resulting in a reversal of wind direction along the line of the loch.

Coire an t-Sith, the fairy hollow, descends from crags near the summit of Beinn Mhór, past 643m Clach Bheinn, and can add to the effect. It ends by pushing debris into the loch, above which is the Paper Cave, narrow boulder caves that have resulted from rock slip.

Nearly opposite, on the east side below 664m Beinn Ruadh, is Loch Eck Caravan Park with moorings for RIBs and other small boats. The nearby Coylet Inn, a 1650 coaching inn, helps attract holidaymakers. In 2017 a hen party staying here used some slices of tree trunk lying on open ground to take a couple of group photos. There was nobody else in the vicinity, but one of the pictures showed a boy looking from behind one of the logs. He was later identified as the Blue Boy, who drowned many years earlier, the colour being how he looked when his body was recovered. The boy and his mother were staying in the inn, where to this day wet footprints appear, footsteps can be heard and objects move, even when no guests are staying. A film, *The Blue Boy*, was made in 1994.

↑ Beinn Bheag on the west side of the loch.

← The hen party with the Blue Boy.

← The Bernice Glen air gap between Beinn Mhór and Meall Breac.

↑ Meall an t-Sith between Coire an t-Sithe and Berenice Glen.

↓ The weir at the end of the loch.

the weir that holds back the loch. This has a vertical drop of perhaps 300mm, although most water goes through a fish pass with low roof in the centre of the weir. There is no warning of the weir.

This is now the River Eachaig with grade 1 rapids as it heads for the Holy Loch, 5km away. Not far downstream is Benmore Botanic Garden, an outstation of Edinburgh's Royal Botanic Gardens, specialising in trees. Its giant 150-year-old redwoods, rhododendrons, a Victorian fernery, shrubs and an enkianthus collection all benefit from 3m of annual rainfall.

A water draw-off point is on the west shore 400m from the end of the loch. The water is used for hydroelectric power generation and as a water supply for Dunoon and other villages.

The chalets of Loch Eck Country Lodges and moored boats are conspicuous at the end of the loch, unlike

DISTANCE_____
10km from Cruach Bhuidhe to Inverchapel

OS 1:50,000 SHEET_____
56 Loch Lomond & Inveraray

LOCH STRIVEN

THINGS THAT COME OUT OF THE SKY

08

The loch was used for testing Barnes Wallis' bouncing bomb before it was used for German dam destruction in the Second World War, but these days it is much calmer.

Having flowed south from its source on Carn Bàn, initially as the Allt Gleann Laoigh, the Balliemore Burn passes standing stones and becomes tidal at the B836. However, there is a small Striven power station at Lochhead, fed by penstocks from east and west. The latter crosses a stepped weir before the loch is reached, low enough to prevent passage by any craft, unless the burn is flowing at least a metre above normal, by which time a dangerous siphon will have developed here.

The route south across Argyll & Bute continues almost as a straight line as Loch Striven divides the Cowal peninsula. Indeed, Loch Fad and Loch Quien hint at a former continuation across Bute.

There is limited roadside parking at Craigendive on the west side of the loch head at the end of the section which drains, leaving a coating of brown wrack. Pheasants give way to mallards, mergansers, herons, cormorants, gannets, oystercatchers and common and black-backed gulls.

The steep sides of the loch are mostly forested, predominantly firs with some deciduous trees such as ash, and landmarks are limited at water level. One of these is the Glentarsan Burn, which

LOCH STRIVEN

↓ Looking down Loch Striven at dawn.

A power station penstock obstructs the tidal Balliemore Burn.

↓ The 405m-high Dun Mòr stands beside the loch.

equipment on long wires, making it unsafe to cross behind them until they are at least 1.5km away. Ordinary fishing vessels are innocuous by comparison.

Peaks on the east side include 458m Cruach nan Caorach, 611m Cruach nan Capull, 381m Sròn Dearg, 522m Black Craig, 472m Blàr Buidhe and 415m Kilmarnock Hill, facing 365m A'Chruach, 405m Dun Mòr, 498m Stùchdan Capuill, 487m Coraddie, 440m Ardbeg Hill, 507m Beinn Bhreac, 451m Sgian Dubh, 486m Meallan Riabhach, 443m Meallan Sidhean and 404m Meallan Glaic.

Gaps between them allow violent squalls to run down off the mountainsides, whipping up water like smoke and sometimes causing clapotis from sets of waves approaching from opposite directions. Seen from Bute, clouds and mists over the loch warn of

descends from Loch Tarsan, held back by two dams. Another is lines of mussel farm floats on the east side.

Tidal streams are weak and the loch is used for storing tankers, but it is a submarine exercise area and is sometimes closed by the Admiralty. Surfaced submarines can tow sonar

approaching bad weather, the loch being known as the Weatherglass of Rothesay.

Tucked in opposite Ardbeg Point is Invervegain at the foot of the windswept Invervegain Glen, another wind funnel. Seals use the loch, as do curlews and eider ducks.

An experimental area is located off Brackley Point, sometimes with buoys joined by wire, followed by the conspicuous NATO Loch Striven Oil Fuel Depot.

Opposite is Strone Point, the hillside above which is partly forested. In the 19th century it was remarkable for having been planted with trees to show the positions of the opposing armies at the Battle of Waterloo.

The loch is joined by the Kyles of Bute, beyond which is Bute, with Ardmaleish Boatbuilding Company's shipyard a prominent structure on its shoreline. From Port Lamont, submarine power cables cross to the island. Extensive floating pipework runs out to fish farm

↑ Squalls can race down each side of Cruach nan Capull.

↓ The NATO fuel jetty on the loch.

↑ Strone Point with the Kyles of Bute to the left.

scale of the operation, now providing no more than a sheltered anchorage for occasional small craft in an area of the loch where the bottom is foul. Barnacles and limpets coat the industrial remains.

The Ardyne Burn joins at the start of Achavoulin Bay, at the other end of which is Toward Quay and the wreck of the 19th-century paddle steamer *Lady Gertrude*, which ran ashore in 1877.

cages anchored in the loch.

Ardyne Point has a pair of disused oil platform fabrication basins. Three concrete gravity platforms were built here in the 1970s by Sir Robert McAlpine, of which the Cormorant A platform for Shell was, at the time, the world's largest ever at more than 300,000 tonnes. The remaining basins do little to indicate the

DISTANCE
17km from Lochhead to Ardyne Point

OS 1:50,000 SHEET
56 Loch Lomond & Inveraray
63 Firth of Clyde

TIDAL CONSTANTS
Rubha Bodach: HW Dover +0100,
LW Dover +0110

SEA AREA
Malin

RESCUE
Inshore lifeboat: Tighnabruaich
All weather lifeboat: Troon

→ The remains of McAlpine's oil rig fabrication yard, now just a sheltered anchorage.

LOCH FYNE

PUFFINS AND SEAFOOD

09

LOCH FYNE

There's naething here but
*   Highland pride,*
And Highland scab and hunger:
If Providence has sent me here,
'Twas surely in an anger.
ROBERT BURNS

A low fall under the old military road bridge above the present A83 bridge is the tidal limit. Fyne Ales Brewery is by the bridge, with Clachan Power Station further back, the flattened valley floor wedged between 658m Clachan Hill and 811m Binnein an Fhìdhleir. Gravel rapids lead down to Loch Fyne, which has acquired a reputation for its seafood and begins with an oyster bar.

Streams in the loch are mostly weak, although stronger off salient points. It is a submarine exercise area, surfaced submarines sometimes towing sonar on wires so that it is necessary to cross at least 1.5km behind. The loch can be sheltered and is mostly forested. Mountain ringlet butterflies are found at high level around the head of the loch

↓ Dunderave Castle sits on Dunderave Point.

↑ The military bridge across the River Fyne at the head of Loch Fyne.

↓ Ardkinglas House and Glen Kinglas.

and Natterer's bats are found down the west shore.

The A83 follows both banks as it rounds the head of the loch. In the eastern direction at Cairndow it departs up Glen Kinglas which is, effectively, an air gap despite the presence of Kinglas Water.

Ardkinglas House was designed in 1907 by Sir Robert Lorimer for Sir Andrew Noble. Ardkinglas Woodland Garden has a noted pinetum, and Gruffalo and Fairy trails. Overshadowing it are 719m Beinn an t-Seilich and 732m Stob an Eas.

A large area of loch in front of the house is covered in floats for growing mussels.

Gleann Beag or Hell's Glen divides Stob an Eas from a ridge dominated by 611m Cruach nam Mult. Across the loch is Dunderave Point. Dunderave Castle was built in 1598 by the MacNaughtons. An unfortunate mistake in the 18th century resulted in a MacNaughton marrying the wrong one of two sisters and eloping to Antrim with the other, when the castle passed to the Campbells of Ardkinglas. It was restored in 1911 by Sir Robert Lorimer and was Neil Munro's Doom Castle. There is a fortified mound in front with assorted animal sculptures and a TV satellite dish by the water.

St Catherines has a jetty from where a passenger ferry can operate to Inveraray. The clear water is occupied by moon jellyfish, oystercatchers, common gulls, herons and wetsuited divers.

The A83 makes another detour around the head of Loch Shira. Conspicuous on Dun Còrr-bhile is Dun na Cuaiche, serving as fort, watchtower and folly.

On the other side it overlooks the River Aray, which joins Loch Shira under the Aray Bridge of 1776. The two 20m masonry spans are separated by an oculus for aesthetics but the steep balustraded bridge struggles to handle A83 traffic with a single lane.

Inveraray Castle, facing the bridge, has been the seat of the Inveraray Campbells since the 15th century. It was rebuilt in the 18th and 19th centuries in Scots baronial style with turreted conical towers, state dining room and drawing room with beautiful ceilings, wall panelling, tapestries and porcelain and an armoury with 1,300 weapons. It has been used in filming *Downton Abbey*.

Inveraray, a former royal burgh, has architecturally noted white buildings from the Georgian planned village, the oldest in Scotland, replacing an older village that was cleared in 1810 as it spoiled

the view from the Duke of Argyll's new castle. The Old Town House was the customs house of 1753. Inveraray Jail is a popular attraction these days. Teetotal Dr Johnson tried whisky for the only time in a local inn and thought it better than English malt brandy. During the Second World War, 250,000 men were trained at HMS Quebec, now home to the

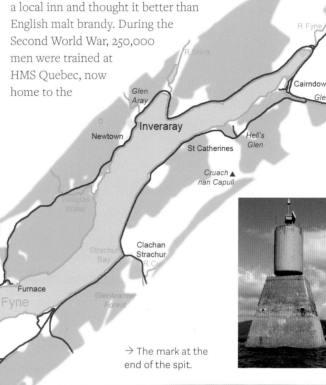

→ The mark at the end of the spit.

→ Aray Bridge over the River Aray by Inveraray Castle.

↑ Clyde Puffer *Vital Spark* and schooner *Arctic Penguin* at Inveraray.

↓ Glenbranter Forest rises behind Strachur Bay.

Argyll Caravan Site. There is an Argyll war memorial on the lochside.

A 500-year-old Celtic cross in Main Street may be from Iona. The Presbyterian church used to have a central dividing wall so that services could be held simultaneously in English and Gaelic, the Gaelic part now being the church hall.

Inveraray Bell Tower reputedly has the finest peal in Scotland and the world's third heaviest peal of ten bells.

In the 19th century there were 250–400 boats landing 15,000–20,000 barrels of Loch Fyne herrings a year here. Para Handy, local author Neil Munro's fictional captain, claimed they were so thick that it was impossible to get the anchor down at times. Now there are two boats permanently at the pier. The *Arctic Penguin* of 1911 is a three-masted iron schooner with a maritime heritage centre inside and the Clyde Puffer *Vital Spark*. This latter name on puffers seems to be becoming almost as common as *Thomas the Tank Engine* on railway engines. The one moored here is actually the *Eilean Eisdeal*, formerly the *VIC 72*, one of the last puffers to be built in 1944, a couple of decades after Munro wrote the last of his *Para Handy* stories.

Beyond Newtown Bay is Newtown at the foot of a hill studded with cairns. Am Buachaille stands at 323m above a caravan site as the Douglas Water joins past a chambered cairn.

A cup and ring-marked rock is found in the trees at Ardnagowan.

Strachur has a dun and the smiddy has been restored as a blacksmith and farrier museum. A circular enclosure may be an early Celtic site. Further attractions are the Strachur Estate bridge of about 1783 and the 1792 church. The village sits in a wind gap, the River Cur dropping to the far side of the village and then flowing away southwards.

Among a small group of houses isolated in the trees at Kenmore Point is a monument. Beyond Pennymore Point is Furnace at the mouth of the Leacann Water. Granite quarries here have paved half of Glasgow but left a block that looks like a castle.

Sandhole, above Whitebridge Bay, suggests varied geology but there is

another disused quarry at the foot of the 420m-high Beinn Ghlas beyond Blackstone Bay.

Crarae Garden, started in 1912 by Lady Grace Campbell of Succoth, is one of the west coast's great gardens, like a Himalayan gorge with rare trees, one of the best rhododendron collections in Scotland and the national collection of

↑ Bàrr an Eich seen from Kenmore.

← Seals resting on the southern extension of Eilean Aoghainn.

↑ Minard Castle faces the loch.

southern beech. There is a chambered cairn and cemetery by Crarae Point.

Across the loch is a chapel site overlooking Kilbride Island. The Strathlachlan River flows into Lachlan Bay past a chapel and the ruin of Old Castle Lachlan. The keep is 15th century and there are sections of wall up to 13m high. All around is Strathlachlan Forest.

The red squirrel was reintroduced to Minard in 1847, spreading from here through the south-west Highlands and north towards Dalmally and Glen Dochart.

Achagoyle Bay and Brainport Bay lead to the Minard Narrows. A 7m black and white-striped round tower with a black framework top marks Paddy rock. Another mark fixes An Oitir as it reaches out to Eilean Aoghainn, which may have had a castle before Castle Lachlan. It is accompanied by the smaller Fraoch Eilean and sometimes by seals and gannets. The 19th-century Minard Castle replaces a 16th-century version between Minard Bay and Union Bay.

A chapel site on the point beyond Creagan Dubh does not have an obvious congregation within sight but platforms in the hillside above must have been cut by someone. Above is 436m Cruach Chuilceachan.

Loch Gair receives some shelter from Ardcastle Wood. Cairns and a square white tower at Pointhouse mark the other side of the mouth.

The Largiemore Burn enters at Largiemore with a pier along the shore.

Glas Eilean helps to shelter Port Ann, which belongs to the Crown.

The Narrows flow to 4km/h (2 knots), ebbing from one hour after Dover high water and flooding from 5h before Dover high water. The fast flow is caused by the Oitir or spit reaching over halfway across the loch from Otter Ferry. The spit has a mark at the end. The ferry ran across the loch until 1948.

From here lower Loch Fyne continues on a larger scale to the Sound of Bute.

DISTANCE
40km from Achandunan to Otter Ferry

OS 1:50,000 SHEETS
50 Glen Orchy & Loch Etive
55 Lochgilphead & Loch Awe
56 Loch Lomond & Inveraray

TIDAL CONSTANTS
Inveraray:
HW Dover +0130, LW Dover +0150
Lochgilphead: HW Dover +0120,
LW Dover +0130

SEA AREA
Malin

RESCUE
Inshore lifeboat: Tighnabruaich
All weather lifeboat: Campbeltown

WEST LOCH TARBERT

LATERAL THINKING WON KINTYRE FOR MAGNUS BAREFOOT

They held unwonted way;–
Up Tarbat's western lake they bore,
Then dragged their bark the isthmus o'er,
As far as Kilmaconnel's shore,
Upon the eastern bay.
SIR WALTER SCOTT

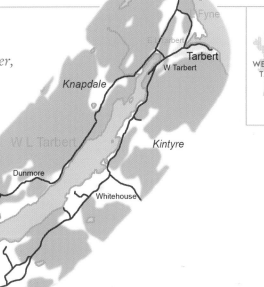

West Loch Tarbert runs south-west from Tarbert, nearly joining up with East Loch Tarbert and separating Knapdale from the Kintyre peninsula. As with a number of other sea lochs in Argyll & Bute, it faces directly into the prevailing headwind.

In the ongoing disputes between the Vikings and the Scots, King Edgar agreed with King Magnus Barefoot that the Scots would have the mainland and the Vikings the islands, islands being defined as anything that Magnus could travel round in his longboat. Magnus sailed round the Kintyre peninsula in 1098 and had his boat dragged 1.4km across the isthmus to complete the circumnavigation and claim Kintyre, something Edgar had certainly not intended. The Vikings retained Kintyre until 1263.

↓ Wrecked fishing boats at West Tarbert.

→ A house at
Dunmore gives a
Nordic feel to the
shoreline.

There is a parking area
by the head of the loch,
overlooked by an aerial.

Flows are barely perceptible
in the loch, but the head
has a very flat bed so it may
be necessary to walk some
distance over hard mud with
worm casts to reach water
deep enough to float a boat.

The West Loch Hotel at
West Tarbert precedes a quay
that handles fishing boats, one of which
lies wrecked in the shallows just to the
north of the quay.

There are standing stones both
sides of the loch and the Abhainn na
Cuile enters on the west side. A modern
cottage looks notably out of place.

Lichened oaks interspersed with fir

trees surround the loch as it widens out.
There is thrift on the rocks above water
level and festoons of wrack and wolf
mussels below, plus oysters and moon
jellyfish, for which this is a breeding
area. Birdlife includes oystercatchers,
cormorants, cuckoos, sandpipers and
hooded crows, which seize mallard chicks

↓ Arriving at
Kennacraig from Islay.

↑ Looking inland up the loch.

as their mothers try to frighten them off.

Eilean dà Ghallagain exhibits small-scale folding of its igneous rock. A pair of islets to the south-west, one topped by a metal post, form a popular hauling out area for seals.

Beyond Eilean Eòghainn, Eilean Ceann na Creige has been linked to the shore to allow it to be used as a car ferry terminal to Port Askaig and to Port Ellen on Islay, a terminal marked by a beacon. Between the terminal and Whitehouse, the peninsula of Eilean Araich Mhòir with its fort has become a resting place for another wreck.

Dunmore on the west side has another fort site and a mausoleum, but the most prominent feature in summer is a display of red hot pokers in the garden of a house standing on the shore. Another house has its own harbour built out of gabion baskets, thoughtfully used as a perch by a heron.

Rock outcrops tend to be small but important in navigational terms. Sgeir Mhein off Rubha Mhein is marked by a red light, while a green light is located off Corran Point, opposite which is the large drying islet of Achadh-Chaorann Bay. Corran Point is at the foot of the distinctively shaped Dùn Skeig hill, which forms the south-western end of the loch and is an obvious site for a vitrified fort. Vegetation includes rhododendrons and yellow irises and provides an environment amenable to vipers. A jetty faces Ferry House but there is no longer a ferry service to disturb the fish basking in the shallows. Birdlife includes eider ducks and black-backed gulls.

Eilean Tràighe and several smaller islets complicate the mouth of the loch, which ends between Ardpatrick Point and Ronachan Point. The ebb starts 6h before Dover high water at up to 2km/h (1 knot) and the flood at Dover high water at up to 1km/h (1 knot).

At the mouth the view changes from the relatively narrow loch to the striking view across the Sound of Gigha to Gigha Island and, beyond it, across the Sound of Jura, to Islay and Jura. The contrast with the creek-like atmosphere of the head of the loch could hardly be greater.

There is a convenient parking area on the A83 to the south of Ronachan Bay.

DISTANCE

15km from Stonfield to Eilean Tràighe

OS 1:50,000 SHEET

62 North Kintyre & Tarbert

TIDAL CONSTANTS

Sound of Gigha:
HW Dover +0340, LW Dover +0420

SEA AREA

Malin

RESCUE

Inshore lifeboat: Campbeltown
All weather lifeboat: Islay

↓ West Loch Tarbert and Dùn Skeig seen from the Sound of Gigha.

LOCH SWEEN

PROBABLY MAINLAND SCOTLAND'S OLDEST CASTLE

Who is he provides this fleet,
At Castle Sween of many hills?
A vigorous man who fears no blast,
His masts up raised, seeking his right.
JOHN MARSDEN

Heading south-west across Knapdale in Argyll & Bute, Loch Sween takes its name from the Suibhne family of Ulster.

Trident-shaped, it is a sea loch, heading directly into the prevailing wind. The longest arm is the most northerly of the three, Caol Scotnish. It is easy for portable craft to launch on to it, but stopping is a problem. The only practical proposition is the passing places on the single track B8025, a practice that is frowned upon despite the light traffic.

Near the head of the loch are a well and cross, hidden in the trees surrounding the water which resembles a pond here. The water, is clear despite the bed of mud and shells. Yellow irises grow around the head of the loch, thrift finds a foothold on the rock outcrops and wracks act as reminders that it is all tidal.

Caol Scotnish is narrow and dotted with islets, but sailing boats do get up this far to moor in this sheltered, idyllic setting. Oystercatchers and herons

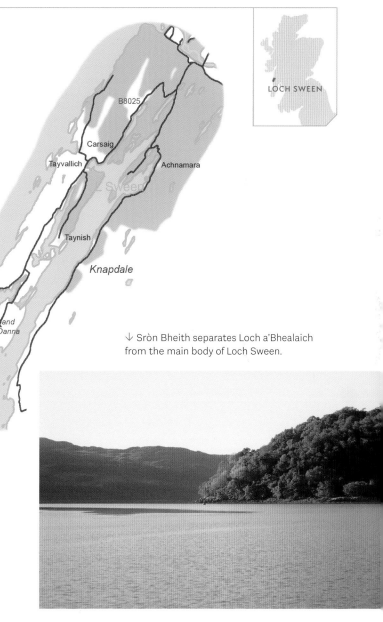

↓ Sròn Bheith separates Loch a'Bhealaich from the main body of Loch Sween.

↓ Moored in Caol Scotnish as mist rises during an autumn dawn.

↓ Looking down Loch Swech past Taynish Island towards the Sound of Jura.

frequent the shallows. Deer browse among the rhododendrons and oaks, but wildcats remain higher up or, at least, hidden.

Flows are imperceptible in the wider part of the loch but quicker in the narrows. Nowhere is narrower than at Scotnish, where a wooden hoist stands on a small jetty, the narrows ending at a picnic area with several parking spaces.

Caol Scotnish widens out into Loch a'Bhealaich, which gives access to Tayvallich, the largest village in the area. Its anchorage was used by the Vikings and later became a herring and lobster fishing centre with a harbour by Telford. It now provides moorings for sailing craft.

Passing the high wooded hill fronted by Sròn Bheith, this joins with the other two arms of Loch Sween. Between these other two is Port Lunna with a marine farm, while the far branch leads up to Achnamara. The former outdoor centre did much pioneering work on helicopter rescue of sea kayak paddlers with regular practical sessions on the loch involving helicopters.

Cala Islet and Eilean Loain are barely distinguishable from the west side of the loch, the tree covering on Eilean Loain blending with the trees on the mainland, although the tree cover reduces steadily towards the coast. The shoreline is rocky but low, ideal for cormorants. Taynish Woods are a fine example of undisturbed coastal oak woods.

On the east side there is an old cross in the woods near Daltote Cottage. The local area was noted for its stone carving in the 14th and 15th centuries.

A round building with a conical roof draws attention to the channel that leads in behind the north end of Taynish Island. This island and the Ulva islands virtually block the mouth of Linne Mhuirich. Although there are at least four routes into the linne, two drain at low water and the others are less than obvious. Equally inconspicuous is the entrance to Ceann an t-Sàilein, an inlet that is now closed off by a very short isthmus carrying the road.

On the east side is another cross, a cairn and a dun, followed by the masterpiece of Castle Sween. Probably the oldest stone castle on the Scottish mainland, it dates from the start of the Norman influence on castle building, while the Vikings were still dominant. The lower rectangular keep dates from the later 12th century. It was ruined by Sir Alexander MacDonald in 1647 with the forces of the Marquess of Montrose and the Highland clansmen supporting the Royalists. It has been further spoilt by a caravan site all around it, and powerboats and water skiers operating from here.

The island of Danna has calcareous rocks with rich flora. Rhizostoma jellyfish swim in the water, eider ducks fly past

↓ Head of Loch Sween and Eilean Loain from above Taynish.

↑ Castle Sween looking impregnable from the loch.

↓ Castle Sween is surrounded by a sea of caravans and, often, by water skiers.

DISTANCE_____
   17km from Arichonan to the Sound of Jura

OS 1:50,000 SHEETS_____
   55 Lochgilphead & Loch Awe
   61 Jura & Colonsay
   62 North Kintyre & Tarbert

TIDAL CONSTANTS_____
   Carsaig Bay: Dover −0610

SEA AREA_____
   Malin

RESCUE_____
   Inshore lifeboat: Tighnabruaich
   All weather lifeboat: Islay

and seals haul out within sight of the powerboats.

Gradually the view opens out from the parallel sides of Loch Sween to take in the panorama of the MacCormaig Isles, the Sound of Jura, Jura itself and, beyond, the higher peaks of Mull, a breathtaking contrast to the intimacy of the head of the loch.

The ebb at the mouth of Loch Sween starts 6h before Dover high water and the flood starts 2h after Dover high water at up to 3km/h (2 knots). Strong south-westerly winds may reverse the ebb.

Danna is only approachable through a locked gate and the minor road on the east side of the loch is some way up the hillside. It is possible to take out at the head of the B8025 at Keillmore, where there is a parking area.

LOCH CRAIGNISH

TRIPLE ATTRACTION

12

Two rows of islands divide Loch Craignish into three parallel channels, offering additional attraction to users. The loch is fed by the Barbreck River, which moves south-west across Argyll & Bute.

The top 300m of the loch drains to leave a spread of wrack, explored by herons, mallards, common gulls and oystercatchers. A south-westerly wind may raise the level of the loch by a metre, while a north-easterly wind can lower it by nearly as much. The south-east side of the loch is mountainous and forested, subject to the occasional passing jet and to severe squalls if the winds are from the east or north-east. Streams are usually up to 2km/h (1 knot), although they may be up to 4km/h (2 knots) at the entrance.

The north-west side is much lower and the shore is followed closely for most of its length by the B8002, but this is a single-track road from which vegetation blocks sight of the loch and there are very few places where it is possible to stop a vehicle and have access to the loch.

Antiquities abound. The A816 near the head of the loch climbs away from Kintraw to the Bealach Mòr past standing

↓ The Barbreck River enters Loch Craignish.

↑ Creag nam Fitheach, from the head of the loch.

↑ Eilean Inshaig with Ardfern Yacht Centre beyond.

↑ The shuttered building on Eilean Mhic Chrion.

↓ Eilean Mhic Chrion is the highest island in Loch Craignish.

stone, cairn and fort sites. Dun na Ban-Oige, variously translated as the fort of the rich woman or young wife, makes good use of the topography for defence.

This is a popular loch with extensive moorings sheltered from most directions. Many sailing boats moor between Eilean Tràighte and Eilean Inshaig and, particularly, around Ardfern Yacht Centre with its pier and slip.

There is a chambered cairn by the end of Eilean Mhic Chrion, the longest island on the north-west side and the highest,

reaching 63m. Halfway down its south-east side is a large brown building, its windows all heavily shuttered.

There are gaps through to the north-west channel at each end of Eilean Dubh with its heather and a dun on Eilean na Nighinn at its north-east end overlooking the Lagoon. Off its other end is an islet used by cormorants and seals.

The largest of the islands is Eilean Righ with three duns, including Dùn Righ, and fish cages down both sides. Eilean nan Gabhar separates it from Island Macaskin, alongside which may be overfalls with southerly winds.

Bàgh Dùn Mhuilig offers very limited room for vehicles to stop by the water and a small beach, although there is more roadside parking a short walk from the water at Kirkton. Around the bay are sited Dun Mhuilig, Craignish Castle, a chapel and graveyard and sculptured stones, also giant hogweed. Red squirrels and deer are

↑ Eilean Dubh beyond Eilean na Nighinn.

↓ Eilean na Nighinn with the north-west channel beyond.

↑ Seals on the islet at the south-west end of Eilean Dubh.

↑ The largest island, Eilean Righ, at the start of the south-east channel.

present, although cattle are more obvious as the loch continues past Bàgh na Cille. Barrel jellyfish float past Port an Lionaidh and Rubh an Lionadh.

There are fine views from Craignish Point with its low cliffs. At hand is Garbh Réisa on the far side of the Dorus Mòr, the great door, which flows at up to 15km/h (8 knots) and is turbulent with it. It claimed the *Comet*, the world's first commerically successful steamship in 1820.

By the end of the loch the road has crossed to the north-west side of the peninsula alongside Loch Beag. The road ends at a farm gate at Aird but continues as a track to the dilapidated high concrete jetty that used to serve Jura. There is a parking area here, but the rocks are high and it is better to land portable craft halfway back to the gate where the rocks are lower.

↓ Garbh Réisa on the far side of the Dorus Mòr with hardly a ripple at the top of a neap tide.

DISTANCE
10km from Craigdhu to Craignish Point

OS 1:50,000 SHEET
55 Lochgilphead & Loch Awe

TIDAL CONSTANTS
Carsaig Bay: Dover −0610

SEA AREA
Malin

RESCUE
Inshore lifeboat: Tighnabruaich
All weather lifeboat: Oban

LOCH MELFORT

A CHALLENGING MARINE PLAYGROUND

13

LOCH MELFORT

From Cruach Narrachan the River Oude flows south-west across Argyll & Bute, through Loch Tralaig to Loch Melfort at Melfort. Swans patrol the peaty waters as it flows into Loch Melfort, lined with deciduous trees and tidal from a minor road bridge. Vehicle access is difficult as the few parking spaces around Fearnach Bay are claimed for a proliferation of holiday houses, not even the jetty being approachable except for customers of the Shower of Herring restaurant. The jetty south of Arduaine is a better bet for users of portable craft intending to explore the loch.

Streams in the loch are imperceptible, but it is exposed to strong winds, especially from the south-west. However, local winds may differ significantly from the general wind direction. The sun can be limited in the afternoon, hidden by 380m Cruach na Seilcheig and 367m Tom Soilleir.

Leading off the head of the loch is Loch na Cille, a small arm with Kilmelford Yacht Haven and 60 moorings

↓ Melfort at the head of Fearnach Bay.

→ Mull's peaks rise beyond Luing.

tucked behind Rubh' an Ròin.

Below Cruach nam Fearna hill is the arm of Rubh' Aird an Stùrra that makes Bàgh na Dalach Dubh-Chlachaich into a wave trap. There are fish farms in Kames Bay, near Creag Aoil and off Eilean Coltair, while Kilchoan Bay has a fish trap site. In the middle of the loch is the low Sgeir na Caillich.

An aerial stands on 257m Beinn Chaorach, at the foot of which is Rubha Àrduaine, conspicuously dark from Loch Melfort and green from Loch Shuna later in the day. An Cnap is topped by Arduaine Garden with spectacular rhododendrons, azaleas, magnolias and other overseas plants.

Eilean Gamhna lies off the point, low but with a prominent nipple in the centre. Beyond, Luing and Shuna are low, but Scarba rises high to the south-west and the peaks of Mull stand to the north-west. Seil Sound and Shuna Sound lead off from the west side and Loch Shuna is to the south. The panorama is of peaks, islands and water, a stunning seascape.

Flows in Loch Shuna start south at

5h 10min after Dover high water and north at 50min before Dover high water at up to 2km/h (1 knot). Asknish Bay is exposed to south-westerly winds. Eilean Creagach rises steeply from the bed of the loch but its shape above water blends in smoothly so that it is surprisingly hard to spot from any direction. Sheltered by Eilean Arsa and Liath Sgeir, Eilean Buidhe, Eilean an Dùin with its fort site and Fraoch Eilean have been connected to form Craobh Marina with more than 500 berths.

↓ Eilean Coltair with Scarba in the distance.

↑ Scarba is seen beyond Shuna.

← Craobh Marina is a leading yachting centre on this coast.

Shuna is one of the Slate Islands. Druim na Dubh Ghlaic rises to 90m and the island has much woodland, the northern two thirds being ringed with trees. Shuna provides excellent sheep grazing and the island's half dozen residents are crofters. Shuna House is the most distinctive building on the island, castellated throughout and with round towers at the corners. There is a jetty between Shuna House and Port an t-Salainn, which is littered with rusting pontoons, and a fish farm.

The trees drop away after Poll na Gile and the coastline becomes more rugged. The strata dip towards the east so this side of the island has a low sloping rock face. At intervals the onshore waves have cut through to form small bays that look out to the south. A cairn stands between Làir Bhan and Shuna Point.

DISTANCE_____
11km from Melfort to Shuna Pt

OS 1:50,000 SHEETS_____
55 Lochgilphead & Loch Awe

TIDAL CONSTANTS_____
L Melfort: Dover −0600

SEA AREA _____
Malin

RESCUE _____
Inshore lifeboat: Tichnabruaich
All weather lifeboat: Oban

↑ Shuna House is the prominent building on Shuna.

↓ The Gulf of Corryvreckan divides Jura from Scarba, Liath Sgeir is in the foreground.

The exposure of Shuna Point to the elements is most graphically illustrated by lines of quartz that run to and fro across the rocks like trails of icing, the harder white quartz standing proud of the softer black igneous rock. From here fast water flows fan out, Shuna Sound, the Sound of Luing, the Gulf of Corryvreckan with the roar of its whirlpool and the Sound of Jura running down the inside of Jura. The southern end of Luing is dwarfed by Scarba. The islands provide an ever-changing panorama and this is a challenging marine playground at its best.

LOCH AWE

THE LONGEST BRITISH LOCH

14

LOCH AWE

*The Awe's fierce stream may
    backward turn,
Ben-Cruachain fall, and crush
    Kilchurn;
Our kilted clans, when blood is high,
Before their foes may turn and fly;
But I, were all these marvels done,
Would never wed the Earlie's son.*

SIR WALTER SCOTT

The lovely young goddess Bheithir preserved her beauty by bathing each night in the magic Well of Youth high on Ben Cruachan. One night she forget to put the capstone back on the spring and in the morning the valley below was filled with Loch Awe. She was punished by the gods who gave her immortality without youth so that she became Cailleach Bheithir, the winter hag, whose icy voice wails around the corries of the peak.

Unfortunately the geological facts do not support the story. Until before the last Ice Age there was a physical divide in the vicinity of Inishail between Ben Cruachan and the main part of Loch Awe. The River Orchy entered the north-east end on its present line and left through the Pass of Brander, as shown by the deep water channel on the loch bed. Removal of the watershed has resulted in a reversal of flows and Loch Awe now empties north-eastwards and then westwards beyond the former watershed.

Ford, now with a bridge, took its name from a former ford that was an important feature on the drove road from Kintaw.

The An Lodan lagoon is the start of Loch Awe where there is a pier and a boat club. Nearby are the remains of the Tower of Caol Chaorunn, which defended the southern approaches to the loch. Now visible are the foundations of a large rectangular building and a round tower. At Torran Mór is a tall cross-carved standing stone, while Dùn Toiseach, the fortress of the chief, was an Iron Age stronghold.

The low hills give way to mountains of increasing height, while wooded outcrops of rock are frequent. Loch Awe is the longest British loch at 41km, running across Argyll & Bute along a fault line. The southern end is wooded on both sides, Inverliever Forest to the north-west

↓ The castle on Innis Chonnell, a stronghold of the Campbells, with Ben Cruachan beyond.

↑ Looking south-west up Loch Awe from the top of the walls of the castle on Innis Chonnell.

and Eredine Forest to the south-east.

At Kilneuair are the remains of St Columba's Chapel of the Yew, roofless but intact inside. It was said to have been built from stones of a 15th century chapel passed from hand to hand by a line of parishioners reaching from Loch Fyne. It has interesting carved stones in the churchyard. A strange feature is the Devil's Handprint, said to have been made by the Devil while making a grab for a tailor who had accepted the challenge to spend a night on the haunted premises.

A line of castles were built along the loch in the 12th and 13th centuries as a defence against Norsemen. Fincharn Castle was built in the 13th century, a MacMartin stronghold until it was set on fire and burnt down by a retainer when the Lord of Fincharn of the day exercised droit de seigneur on his wedding night.

A cairn stands near to the castle.

Liever Island stands at the mouth of the River Liever, with conspicuous greenhouses. Next to the ruins of Inverliever church is the Sun Stone with a series of radiating lines.

Roads run along both shores, the one on the east being slightly more major and nearer the shoreline, but the one on the west is still near enough for a car to have crashed upside down on the rocks by the water's edge. The wreck is now covered with ivy. The first of five forest walks shows alternative woodland views from this road.

Loch Awe is very deep, exceeding 90m off Innis Stùire. As befits such a deep loch, it has a monster, Beathach Mór, a giant serpent with a horse-like head and a dozen huge scaly legs. The loch has pieces of wood that seem to float vertically with just their ends showing, assuming they are just wood...

Mystery surrounds St Mochoe of Nendrum's early Christian cille at Rubha na Fidhle, fiddler's point, near Milmaha. Here there are broken headed crosses, granite outcrops with two carved figures and Pictish mirror symbols. It is one of the earliest ecclesiastical sites around the loch, and certainly dates to no later than the 5th century.

Opposite, at Braevallich, activity is right up to date with a large fish farm protected by a wall of floating tyres and a high fence preventing access to the road. The Abhainn a' Bhealaich river discharges into the loch.

Devil's Rock, an erratic boulder by the Kames River, was said to have been thrown by the Devil to stop the noise of people disturbing his peace on Sundays with their worshipping. A ruined fort near the foot of the valley also tried to keep the peace.

Innis Sèa-Ràmhach has the remains of a 14th-century chapel. A pier opposite at Newyork was built in the 18th century as one of the earliest speculative developments by the York Building Co, not with any great success.

Innis Chonnell has the vast remains of a 13th-century castle, which was the stronghold of the Campbells until the mid-15th century and was later used as

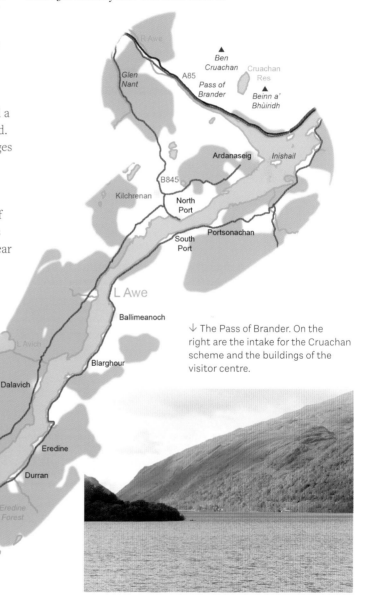

↓ The Pass of Brander. On the right are the intake for the Cruachan scheme and the buildings of the visitor centre.

a prison. The stonework is largely still intact, including the dungeons and a great fireplace.

There was a mill located at Ardchonnell in the 17th century.

Dalavich is a village built by the Forestry Commission in 1952. The River Avich is followed by the Sreang Lathurnach, the string of Lorn, an ancient bridleway running west to Kilmelford. An osprey viewpoint is established near Kilmun.

Among the wonders of Loch Awe are the 27m falls on the Allt Blarghour when it is in spate. Today there is little left of the once thriving township of Blarghour nearby. Beyond the Allt Beochlich is Ballimeanoch. The Abhainn Fionain is another significant tributary on the west side.

Meadows sweep down to the water just before South Port. One of the narrowest points on the loch, it used to have a ferry operating from here across to North Port until 1945. Portsonachan Hotel was built on the drove road in the 19th century.

Kilchrenan has a 17th century church built on 13th century foundations. Its graveyard has carved memorial stones of the Loch Awe School, twin stemmed foliage with an entwined warrior.

Power lines cross the loch in a single span and the Cladich River enters as the loch reaches its former head. The cleft continues past conspicuous Kilchurn Castle and into Glen Strae, but the 1,126m high Ben Cruachan towers over all as the front marker in an area of high peaks beyond the north-west end of Loch Awe. The former watershed is marked by the Black Islands and Inishail, the latter with the remains of the church founded in the 7th century.

The length of Loch Awe means that the waves have considerable fetch and can prove very difficult as the loch runs along the line of the prevailing wind. Turning the corner ought to bring shelter, but the Pass of Brander can funnel winds through here.

Ardanaiseig was a 19th-century Campbell mansion, which has since become a hotel.

At Tervine a fish farm is surrounded by floats supporting lines that can be hard to see.

On the north side are the intakes for the Cruachan pumped storage scheme,

one of the most ambitious hydroelectric power schemes in the world at 440MW. Through a tunnel down in the heart of the mountain is a vast wood-panelled machine room with four great turbines. These use off-peak surplus electricity from conventional power stations to pump water from the loch, 370m to Cruachan Reservoir. This water, added to by surface sources, is then used to drive the turbines to supply peak power requirements.

The northern edge of the loch acts as a transport corridor. The single track Glasgow to Oban railway line, the Callander & Oban Railway of 1880, has an unusual signalling system with pairs of semaphore home signals at very frequent intervals, usually raised for both directions simultaneously. In the gap between the railway and the loch runs the A85, in places space being at such a premium that the road is cantilevered out over the loch.

The Pass of Brander was part of an important drove route. A waterfall drops from Lochan na Cuaig on the south side of the pass. Just to its north is a cave used by the Irish mercenary MacFadyen, a hireling of Edward I, and his bodyguard of 15 after his huge invading army was routed by William Wallace in 1297.

A safety line and warning notices stop boats coming too close to the barrage, which is used to raise the level of the loch for hydroelectric power purposes. The barrage includes a fish lift and an electronic fish counter. The River Awe falls at 0.5% through a valley of Carboniferous conglomerate hard enough to give interesting rapids. There is limited roadside parking. Management of the barrage has often resulted in inadequate water levels below the barrage and flooding of properties upstream.

Cairns near the barrage cover the graves of men killed in the battle of 1308 when Robert the Bruce reversed the outcome of the Battle of Tyndrum two years earlier by routing John MacDougall of Lorn.

↑ North Port, seen from South Port. Ben Cruachan rises at the back.

DISTANCE
37km from Ford to the Pass of Brander

OS 1:50,000 SHEETS
50 Glen Orchy
55 Lochgilphead & Loch Awe

15

LOCH ETIVE

REMOTE WITH A STING IN THE TAIL

LOCH ETIVE

To where Dunstaffnage hears the raging
Of Connal with his rocks engaging.
SIR WALTER SCOTT

The River Etive becomes tidal at Kinlochetive, a point that can be reached down Glen Etive by vehicle using a 20km single track road. After this there is no road for 15km, making it a wonderfully remote piece of water with dramatic scenery. Unfortunately, midges have no problems getting here. Another possible encounter is the Fàchan of Glen Etive, a monster with one eye, one arm from his chest and one leg.

The derelict pier at the head of the loch has been renovated and is being used to ship out timber from Glenetive Forest.

Winds are erratic or blow along the loch. Flows are negligible to the Bonawe Narrows, although the scenery is dramatic and the shoreline steep as far as this point. The Allt a' Bhiorain also joins

the head of the loch past 590m Meall nan Gobhar as it starts a ridge that rises up to 839m Beinn Trilleachan, with the Trilleachan Slabs at 40°, which are much enjoyed by rock climbers. Facing across the loch is 1,078m Ben Starav with its golden eagles and steep sides that sweep down to the water. Ben Starav has notable dry clefts of boulders where spates have gouged out channels. Looking back up the glen shows more stark peaks.

Oak, birch and hazel trees, bracken and bluebells cover the lower flanks, where deer, tree pipits, redstarts and warblers can be found, with herons and seals in the loch itself.

Each side of 800m Stob an Duine Ruaidh a significant stream enters the Allt Coire na Làrach after Rubha Doire

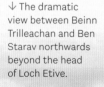

↓ The dramatic view between Beinn Trilleachan and Ben Starav northwards beyond the head of Loch Etive.

↓ An indication of the savage power unleashed when water floods down off Ben Starav.

Làrach and the Allt Ghiusachan at Inverghiusachan Point.

A pier, moorings and boathouses serve a couple of cottages at Barrs in the most remote part of the loch. Some pillow lava edges Rubha Bharr. Beyond the point is Bàgh na Dalach, into which the Allt Easach and Abhainn Dalach discharge.

The wider River Kinglass enters Ardmaddy Bay beyond the relative plateau of 439m Monadh Liath and the River Liver joins Inverliver Bay. A further tributary on this side is the River Noe into Port an Dòbhrain, backed by the highest mountain in the area, Ben Cruachan.

By comparison, the Cadderlie Burn flowing from 578m Meall Dearg to Camas na Cùirte is less extreme. The peaks on the west side step back up to 714m with Beinn Mheadhonach, although 555m Beinn Duirinnis is more dramatic for being closer.

↑ Woods alongside the loch towards Barrs.

↑ Glen Noe runs down behind Ben Cruachan.

→ Pillow lava rolls into the loch.

↓ The heart of the Bonawe Furnace complex.

Heather grows beside the loch.

Both sides of the loch have been used for quarrying. Industry now includes mussel floats around Rubh' Àird an Droighinn. Bonawe Quarry exports crushed granite and, formerly, top-quality setts, including those for Glasgow's King George V Bridge and for the entrance to the original Mersey Tunnel.

Dun Mor can be found as a mound at the mouth of the River Awe. The river, partly obstructed by tree debris, produces a spit. With Eilean Duirinnis, now a peninsula, the loch is forced through the Bonawe Narrows. Named from the Gaelic Bun Atha, mouth of the Awe, the gap was formerly the only crossing point for the loch. The ferry has gone, leaving an awkward break in the B845 and only high power lines across the water.

Inverawe Smokehouse is on one bank of the Awe, facing across to Bonawe Furnace, the most complete charcoal-fuelled ironworks in Britain, an Ancient Monument. The furnace was operated from 1753 to 1876 by Furness ironmasters

who used local oak and birch for charcoal and shipped ore from Ulverston to use with local limestone, exporting pig iron to Cumbria and making cannon balls for use in the Napoleonic wars. Lorn Furnace employed 600 people. Its bellows were powered by a breast shot waterwheel fed from the River Awe and it had an early tramway with tracks of slate. Kelly's Pier of 1753 is named after Alexander Kelly, who leased the furnace. A drystone structure 120m long and 6.1m wide, the pier was used by the Newland Company of Furness to unload the iron ore and there are the remains of a timber extension that would have been used for steamships.

Flows begin out through the narrows from 3h before Dover high water at up to 3km/h (2 knots) and in from 3h 50min after Dover high water at up to 5km/h (3 knots).

There are tidal ponds at the back of Airds Bay. The River Nant enters through

↓ The loch cuts between Ben Cruachan and Beinn Duirinnis.

↑ Rapids forming off the jetty at Taynuilt.

↓ Off Kilmaronaig the ebb is already moving fast. These pictures were taken at spring tides but in calm conditions.

deposited debris to fill in its side of the loch. Fish cages and mussel floats are anchored along the side of the loch in the clear water. A jetty and moorings lead to the mouth of the Allt Nathais.

A jetty serves Ardchattan Priory Gardens. The priory of St Catan, a follower of St Columba, was established in 1231. Robert the Bruce held a Parliament here in 1308, the last in Gaelic.

Near St Baodan's church is a well that grants penny wishes at the foot of the 350m rounded bulk of Na Maoilean.

The railway follows the shoreline to Connel. There is a pier at the back of the bay sheltered by Rhuba a' Chàirn Bhig. Facing Linne na Craige or Stonefield Bay and taking some shelter from Abbot's Isle are Achnacloich Gardens.

The low Moss of Achnacree extends across much of the loch from the foot of 308m Beinn Lora. Dotted with cairns, it has been used for peat cutting.

From the Kilmaronaig narrows the water gets serious, an indication of what is to come. The southern half of the narrows are obstructed by islets and flows run to 11km/h (6 knots), out from 3h 20min before Dover high water and in from 3h 40min after Dover high water. An eddy forms on the south-west side on the ebb, and a race and eddy form on the south-east side with the flood. Kelp waves as the water boils.

The velocity eases for a while in Connel Sound. Black Crofts face Dunfuinary with a house and round tower. The church in Connel has stained glass showing the bridge and the Falls of Lora. Just upstream is an old jetty, which offers little practical help.

Taynuilt, where the houses are of granite from Inverawe Quarry. Station buildings house the West Highland Brewery and Shore Cottage, now Robin's Nest Tea Room. A windfarm shows on the skyline near Loch Nant.

For centuries there was a 3.7m granite pillar near Airds Bay House to St Nessog. Furnace workmen moved it to Taynuilt in 1805 and set it up as the first monument in Britain to Nelson – it was positioned before Nelson's funeral.

Airds Point is steep but faces the mouth of the River Esragan, which has

Connel Bridge of 1903 is of particular value as a marker of the falls. The flows were too strong for the piers to be in the water so they are 160m apart and lean inwards. There is 15m clearance over the water beneath the bridge.

The Falls of Lora are formed by a ledge just upstream from the bridge, starting near the north bank and reaching more than halfway across the sound. At low water springs there is a 1.5m fall over the ledge. Most of the water passes on the south side. On the ebb there is a chute on the north side used by white water kayaks. This meets the main flow from the south side below the bridge to form a line of standing waves and boils that continue for 1km beyond Ledaig Point.

On the flood there is a wide area of broken water over the ledge. Flows are

↑ The Falls of Lora at Connel Bridge during the ebb. The rock shelf is clearly visible beyond the bridge.

↓ Highland cattle by Linne na Craige.

↑ The flood over the Falls of Lora seen from Connel Bridge. The broken water is over the central rock shelf.

DISTANCE_____
19km from Gualachulain to Ardmucknish Bay

OS 1:50,000 SHEETS_____
49 Oban & East Mull
50 Glen Orchy & Loch Etive

TIDAL CONSTANTS_____
Bonawe:
HW Dover −0320, LW Dover −0300
Connel: Dover −0510
Dunstaffnage Bay: Dover −0520

SEA AREA _____
Malin

RESCUE _____
Inshore lifeboat: Loch Lomond
All weather lifeboat: Oban

officially up to 11km/h (6 knots), but some claim they exceed 15km/h (8 knots). There is no slack water. The tide goes out from 3h 20min before Dover high water and in from 3h 20min after Dover high water. However, times can vary by as much as an hour and a half. They are more often early if there is a westerly wind and low pressure and later with the opposite conditions. The advice is to pass within an hour of the turn of the tide and to be aware that stopping on the east side of the bridge to inspect is not easy. Once ashore, however, there are good viewpoints from the A85 to the west of the bridge and from the A828 on the bridge itself.

The shoreline at North Connel is occupied by Oban Airport with gliding at the Connel Flying Club. The tide drops to leave a wide shingle area at Ledaig Point, the southern end of Ardmucknish Bay.

Camas Bruaich Ruaidhe or Salmore Bay has moorings and a fish farm, but most of the moorings are in Dunstaffnage Bay, where there is a marina with a slip and shelter from Eilean Mòr and the rocks of Eilean Beag. At the back of the bay are the large premises of the Scottish Association for Marine Science.

A jetty stands by Dunstaffnage Castle. The capital of the kingdom of Dalriada was here or hereabouts and the Stone of Destiny, now in Westminster, was brought from Tara and built into the castle wall until 843. The present building was started in the 13th century by the MacDougalls, the Lords of Lorn, and was used by Alexander III as a base to drive the Vikings out of the Hebrides.

LOCH CRERAN

FROM TRAINS TO CARS TO CYCLES

Lament, O, Glen-Creran, Glen-Duror, Ardshiel,
High offspring of heroes, who conquer'd were never,
For the deeds of your fathers no bard shall reveal,
And the bold clan of Stuart must perish for ever!
JAMES HOGG

The head of Loch Creran is quieter than in the past, when the A828 passed over the bridge at the tidal limit, where the River Creran enters at Glasdrum. The bridge at Caolas Creagan shortens the road journey significantly and cyclists are now the main users of the road on the south side of the first part of the loch.

The sides of the loch are largely wooded with Glasdrum Wood and Barcaldine Forest rising steeply at first on the sides of 937m Beinn Sgulaird, 968m Meall Garbh and 549m Beinn Churalain. Breaks in the trees along the shoreline are occupied by foxgloves, bracken, gorse, broom, heath and grassland with thrift and wrack in the tidal zone, the latter clearly visible as over a kilometre drains at the head of the loch. There are pine martens, oystercatchers, chequered skippers and other rare butterflies, plus the rather more common midge.

An ancient burial ground is sited clear of the treeline, high above a conspicuous modern house on the north shore.

Flows are imperceptible in the upper loch until Caolas Creagan,

← The prominent Inver boathouse beside the upper loch.

where they can reach 9km/h (5 knots). They start out 5h before Dover high water, with overfalls on the north side for 1km, and return from 1h 40min after Dover high water. Passing over them is the A828 bridge, replacing a former railway bridge.

↑ Looking back up the loch towards the Caolas Creagan from Rubha Garbh.

Barcaldine Marine has 100 moorings and a pier with some commercial shipping moored in the loch. On the other side of Rubha Dearg the Dearg Abhainn flows into the loch.

The Scottish Sea Life Sanctuary features sharks, seal rescue and fish-farming techniques, there being several marine farms in the loch. In the woods behind are a standing stone and a cairn.

There is a Rubha Garbh on each side of the loch. Above Rubha Mòr is the 17th-century Barcaldine Castle, 6km from Barcaldine itself.

Loch Creran used to have a prolific herring fishing industry. The main current fish interest is Scottish Sea Farms at South Shian with a long floating jetty and a private slipway. This is the last publicly accessible point on the loch for portable craft, with limited parking.

As well as the usual food and drink, the Creagan Inn offers showers and a view that includes rocks used by seals and eider ducks. The clear water has moon and lion's mane jellyfish. Although serpulid worms are common around Britain, the periphery of Loch Creran is the only place where they form reefs.

An Iola enters on the north side and, beyond an aerial opposite, the Abhainn Teithil descends from Barcaldine Forest, as do cycle trails.

Beyond Rubha Riabhach there are two routes to the Lynn of Lorn, one each side of Eriska isle.

Small craft can pass to the south of Sgeir Caillich where cormorants watch

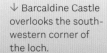

↓ Barcaldine Castle overlooks the south-western corner of the loch.

over the accelerating water by a private jetty as bootlace weed lashes. Native deciduous trees make up Shian Wood. A crannog site at the south-east corner of Eriska can draw some protection from the flows in An Doirlinn, out from 5h 50min before Dover high water and in from 40min after Dover high water at up to 7km/h (4 knots), although the channel largely dries with a causeway at low water. Craft are also inconvenienced by the Isle of Eriska Bridge, built at the turn of the 20th century with ornamental iron gates that can be used to close the bridge. Beyond Rubha Mór there is open water in the Lynn of Lorn.

Larger craft need to pass North Shian and round Rubha nam Faoileann at the northern end of Eriska. Flows in this larger channel are equally swift, out from 5h 40min before Dover high water and in from 30min after Dover high water. Entry to the Lynn of Lorn is dotted with islets, Dearg Sgeir, Glas Eilean and Branra Rock, the latter marked by an iron cage with an artificial reef built on its west side.

Eilean Dubh is prominent in the centre of the Lynn of Lorn and, beyond Lismore and Loch Linnhe, the Kingairloch mountains form a solid backdrop.

DISTANCE
14km from Glasdrum to Eilean Dubh

OS 1:50,000 SHEETS
49 Oban & East Mull
50 Glen Orchy

TIDAL CONSTANTS
L Creran Head: HW Dover −0500, LW Dover −0430
Barcaldine Pier: HW Dover −0500, LW Dover −0450
Port Appin: HW Dover −0520, LW Dover −0540

SEA AREA
Malin

RESCUE
Inshore lifeboat: Loch Lomond
All weather lifeboat: Oban

↑ Beinn Mòlurgainn and Beinn Bhreac on the south side of the loch.

↓ An Doirlinn looking towards the Isle of Eriska Bridge with Kingairloch peaks in the distance.

LOCH LEVEN

17 LOCH LEVEN

ALUMINIUM SMELTING AND THE MELTING POT
FOR CLAN ATROCITIES

The Campbells are comin, Oho, Oho!
The Campbells are comin, Oho, Oho!
The Campbells are comin to Bonie Lochleven,
The Campbells are comin, Oho, Oho!
ROBERT BURNS

Kinlochleven has long held importance as the bridging point on the River Leven. Any long journey not involving boats needed to travel the greater part of both sides of Loch Leven, the whole of what is now the B863. There are grade 3 rapids downstream of the bridge and tidal water reaches to them.

Additional importance came to the village in 1908 in the form of an aluminium smelter. Construction required a 10km cableway, a temporary railway and a temporary power station. Water was plentiful, 142mm of rain falling in one 24-hour period during construction. One of the first hydroelectricity-powered smelters, it was supplied by six penstocks 280m long, the Pelton wheels producing 21MW. The smelter was closed in 1996 and the power station now feeds the national grid, discharging its spent water into the river upstream of the bridge. There is an Aluminium Story visitor centre.

Water is supplied from the Blackwater Reservoir, formed by damming the River Leven. Dubh Lochan has survived downstream of the reservoir, but much of the river's flow is now piped.

Further significance has come to the village with the establishment of the West Highland Way long-distance path, this being one of the few villages it passes on this part of its rugged course.

↓ The River Leven in Kinlochleven.

The water is peaty but clear. Loch Leven flows westwards to Loch Linnhe, mostly at less than 2km/h (1 knot). It is joined by the Allt Coire na Bà on the west side of Kinlochmore, the village on the north side of the river. Portable craft are best launched from the south side of the loch on the west side of Kinlochleven; a moderate walk is needed along a paved footway.

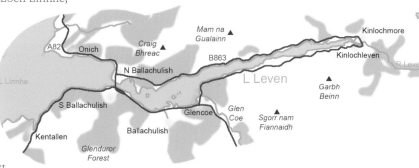

The loch is sheltered from the north and south, especially over its eastern half, with mountains rising steeply from the loch, making it gloomy, especially in the morning before the sun rises above the mountains. On the south side these include 867m Garbh Bheinn, Meall Garbh just a metre lower, Sgòrr nam

↓ Sgòrr nam Fiannaidh and the Pap of Glencoe.

↓ The Pap of Glencoe, Sgòrr nam Fiannaidh and, beyond Glencoe village, Buachaille Etive Mòr.

Fiannaidh running up to 967m and the distinctive quartzite Sgorr na Ciche (the Pap of Glencoe) at 742m. Facing on the north side are the Mamore Forest peaks, dominated by 764m Beinn na Caillich, running on to 796m Mam na Gualainn. There are deciduous woods along the north shore with gorse adding colour.

There is also a fish farm on the north side on the approach to the Caolas

nan Con, marked by a decaying timber beacon. Flows pick up here to 8km/h (4 knots) outwards from 4h 20min before Dover high water and to 11km/h (6 knots) inwards from 2h 40min after Dover high water. Beyond this point flows are weak.

A graveyard and a jetty are located at the back of Camas na h-Eirghe. The mountainsides become more extensively forested as the loch opens out at the

River Coe confluence. The view up Glen Coe takes in peaks including 1,115m Stob Coire nan Lochan. By the shore is the village of Glencoe with a pier and the Glencoe & North Lorn Folk Museum.

Callert House is at the end of the Lairig Mor, a coffin road, not the easiest of routes to walk even without a coffin.

The Eilean a' Chòmhraidh led to Eilean Munde or St Mungo's. The chapel remains are from about 600, built by St Fintan Mundus. Each clan had its own landing, the Ports of the Dead, to reach the ancient burial ground. The island was used as a cemetery to prevent wolves from digging up bodies.

Ballachulish, where the River Laroch enters the south side of the loch, developed with slate workings. The quarries have been disused since the 1950s and are partially landscaped. A couple of artificial harbours were excavated and Rubha na Glas-lice is of debris from slate workings. Highland Mysteryworld now attempts to attract visitors to the area.

The Glen Duror Forest mountains rise high behind the village. On the north sides the peaks taper down from Craig Bhreac at 615m.

Marine farms are located on both sides of the low green Eilean Choinneich. A mausoleum is located among the heather above Rubha Charnuis, a raised beach that shelters the loch from the west. Eilean na h-luraiche provides further shelter for Poll an Dùnain, which is also known as Bishop's Bay.

In the centre of the loch is a 36m-deep hole. To its west is a bar, with as little as 3m depth as the water approaches the Loch Leven Narrows. Kelp waves in flows to 10km/h (5 knots), out from 4h 20min before Dover high water and in from 1h 50min after Dover high water with little slack water.

Ferry slipways can be reached on both sides of the narrows, but the A82 no longer uses them and has been taken over the Ballachulish Bridge since 1974. Of

← Glen Duror Forest overlooks the lower loch.

→ The Ardgour peaks beyond the Ballachulish Bridge.

294m total length, it is a continuous steel structure with a 183m main span giving 17m clearance. Caolas Mhic Phadruig is 7m deep under the bridge, but this drops to less than 3m again at another bar to the west of the bridge. There can be a race on the ebb with overfalls when the wind is westerly. A spring tide can produce an eddy in front of North Ballachulish in Camas a' Chòis.

South-westerly winds can bring a considerable swell and southerly winds result in heavy squalls off the mountains. However, streams are weak as Ballachulish Bay leads out into Loch Linnhe.

There are cairns on both sides of the loch near the bridge and a Stuart memorial. North Ballachulish has a confectionery factory. The Ballachulish Hotel on the south side accompanies the Dragon's Tooth Golf Course.

Between the remains of an old pier and some pillow lava at Rubh' a' Bhaid Bheithe in Great Wood of Lettermore is a memorial stone to James Stewart, James of the Glen, hanged here after a false allegation of the murder in 1752 of Colin Campbell of Glenure, the government factor for the Cameron and Stewart estates forfeited after the 1745 uprising.

Portable craft might be taken out at Onich. The pier, along from the Clach-a-Charra site, is privately owned, but there is a beach below the A82 next to the Onich Hotel. The Onich Tearoom also offers refreshments. From any of these places there are fine views across Loch Linnhe to the Ardgour peaks and down to the Kingairloch mountains.

DISTANCE
16km from Kinlochleven to Rubh' a' Bhaid Bheithe

OS 1:50,000 SHEETS
41 Ben Nevis

TIDAL CONSTANTS
L Leven Head: Dover −0440
Corran: HW Dover −0510,
LW Dover −0520

SEA AREA
Malin

RESCUE
Inshore lifeboat: Loch Lomond
All weather lifeboat: Oban

LOCH LAGGAN

SANDY BEACHES BETWEEN THE ROCKS

The Allt a' Chaoil-réidhe rises on Ben Alder and flows northwards as the River Pattack before deflecting sharply westwards and flowing to the River Lochy through Glen Spean. Gradually the river deepens and slows, opening out into Loch Laggan at Kinloch Laggan between an ancient church and an area of sandbanks that emerge when the loch is drawn down.

Places to reach the loch are limited. One of the best is a lay-by beside the River Pattack just before it enters the loch. When conditions are suitable this is used to climb down the low bank and ford the river to reach the popular extensive sand area at the head of the loch. More lay-bys follow, but they are small and lead to wooded slopes which are much higher. By Aberarder Lodge,

LOCH LAGGAN

Aberarder Forest

A86

Kinloch Laggan

Aberarder

L Laggan

R Pattack

Moy Forest

Moy Lodge

Ardverikie Forest

R Spean

Lochan na h-Earba

↓ Looking up Loch Laggan to Binnein Shios.

DISTANCE
11km from Kinloch Laggan to Moy Lodge

OS 1:50,000 SHEET
42 Glen Garry & Loch Rannoch

Highland All Terrain have 4x4 and quad bike hire options available.

If the prevailing wind is blowing then waves will be largest at this end of the loch, although the sides of the loch are protected by an avenue of peaks. The highest is Creag Meagaidh on the north side, although the most conspicuous is Binnein Shios which blocks out its higher neighbour, Binnein Shuas. Loch Laggan (Celtic for hollow) forms an almost straight cleft between lofty peaks.

A single sailing boat may lie at anchor at Tullochroam. On a still day with the peaks and clouds reflected in the water, it is a truly fabulous place to be in solitude. Surprisingly, the loch is relatively shallow, being under 10m deep throughout.

Of the few houses to be seen, the most magnificent is at Ardverikie, more of a castle with lighter coloured stone courses spiralling up the round tower in one corner to the pointed roof. There used to be a castle on an island in the middle of the loch, but now only the remnants of stone walls still stand.

Near it, a river brings in water from Lochan na h-Earba, flowing in between the lichen-covered birches on the south side of the loch. Mostly, though, the trees are planted firs, but they are rather spasmodic in Aberarder Forest on the north side. Aberarder itself is on a rare flatter area of land where the Allt a'

↓ Ardverikie on the remote south side of the loch.

Chrannaig enters the loch. The Creag Meagaidh nature reserve has parking and, unusually, overnight stopping is permitted.

The bridge over the Allt Coire Ardair and Allt a' Choire Chomharsain is followed by a wider section of verge from where it is possible to walk across flat ground to reach the loch's edge.

The upper waterfall of the Allt Coire Choille-rais is conspicuous after rain as it drops over the shoulder in Moy Forest. Just after its entry to the loch a single motorboat may be moored off a ruined boathouse.

Moy Lodge signals the end of Loch Laggan and the start of the River Spean. The river begins amid sandbanks, the banks of the loch having been mostly of rock boulders since Kinloch Laggan. Here it is a totally different river from what it is to become further down and perhaps from what it once was in days before its level was dam regulated.

↑ The view up Loch Laggan to the island that once had a castle.

↓ Looking down Loch Laggan to Binnein Shios from where the River Pattack enters.

19 LOCH LOCHY

BELOW GLENGARRY'S BOWLING GREEN

LOCH LOCHY

On the airy Ben-nevis the wind is awake;
The boat's on the shallow, the ship on the lake.
Ah! now in a moment my country I leave;
The next I am far away, far on the wave.
O! fare thee well, fare thee well, Glen-n-h'Albyn,
O! fare thee well, fare thee well, Glen-n-h'Albyn.
ANON

Loch Lochy is 16km long and 160m deep, the very essence of Glen Albyn as it cuts dead straight between steeply rising shores. A reputed monster, Lizzie, seems even less likely than the one to the north-east in Loch Ness, at the other side of the Caledonian Canal.

The canal's construction included raising the top water level of the loch by 3.7m. The two Laggan Locks drop the canal down from its summit level and out of the Laggan Avenue reach, a section of canal thickly lined with pines. This 2km stretch, crossed by power lines, is the only section of canal without a natural watercourse alongside.

Wooden chalets follow the graveyard beside the Kilfinan Burn where it enters the Ceann Loch, the mausoleum of the Chiefs of Glengarry. In 1544, 300 Frasers

↓ Looking up Glen Albyn past Ruighe na Beinne.

and Macintoshes fought 600 Macdonalds and Camerons here in the Battle of the Shirts, so called because the clansmen stripped off in the sunshine before the combat commenced. Only a dozen were left standing afterwards.

South Laggan Forest on both banks provided conifers for Corpach Paper Mill. It becomes Clunes Forest on the northwest bank. Above is the treeless Glengarry Forest, including the 901m cone of Ben Tee, fairy hill, 887m Sean Mheall and 935m Sròn a' Choire Ghairbh,

rough corrie nose, all part of Glengarry's Bowling Green. Birdlife by the loch varies from sandpipers to raptors.

General Wade's Military Road, the line of a dismantled railway, the A82 and power lines all leave from beside Loch Lochy via Glen Gloy, about two thirds of the way down its length. The River Gloy doubles back after incising a deep cleft parallel to Loch Lochy. The river looks as if it formerly flowed into Loch Lochy some 3km further south-west.

↑ Pines along the shoreline at Bunarkaig.

↑ Forestry taking place above Glenfintaig House.

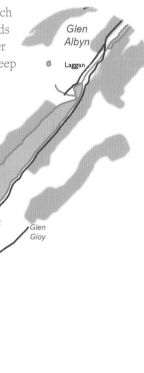

↑ An inlet at Bunarkaig facing Ben Nevis.

↓ The Càm Bhealach leaves the loch below Sean Mheall.

A concrete platform on the west shore was built for Second World War commando training attacks. Most of this activity was based around Bunarkaig near where the River Arkaig enters from Loch Arkaig, opposite an obelisk in the trees. This is the only place where the narrow loch widens.

To Gairlochy the loch narrows into the Caledonian Canal as it leaves in the natural course of the river. The route was considered by Captain Burt in 1726. It was surveyed by James Watt in 1773 when it was believed the sea level was not the same at each end. The River Lochy arrives in a new Mucomir Cut, having picked up the River Spean at Bridge of Mucomir. A hydro-electric power station was added at the confluence with the Spean in the 1960s.

DISTANCE
15km from Ceann Loch to Gairlochy

OS 1:50,000 SHEETS
34 Fort Augustus, Glen Roy & Glen Moriston
(41 Ben Nevis)

LOCH ARKAIG

REMOTE SCOTLAND WITH PLENTY OF VISITORS

20

This shepherd's house, a century ago,
Got meal twice yearly, boated up the loch.
And yet his family made their own world here.
JOHN HARGREAVES

LOCH ARKAIG

Although the head of the loch is one of the remoter areas in Scotland, the frequent grassy slopes down to Loch Arkaig make it seem more domesticated than some. A minor road follows the north shore of the loch to an unexpected car park and tents, a gathering place for walkers. This is in a geological rift with Loch Morar, from the direction of which the River Pean flows to meet the River Dessary above the head of the loch. There are also routes to Loch Cuaich, Loch Garry and Loch Shiel. The soldiers in the former Strathan barracks at the head of the loch were probably less enthusiastic about the location. The accommodation was little more than a cottage, built following the 1745 uprising.

The loch runs east across the Highlands for 18km, usually about 1km wide. This part of Lochaber is partially wooded, including fragments of ancient Caledonian pine forest, and partially covered in rough sheep grazing, alders, birches and bracken.

Osprey, guillemots, herons, Canada geese and great northern divers can be seen here, as well as red deer, polecats and, of course, midges. As recently as 1857 Lord Malmesbury was given a

↓ Looking up Glen Pean from the head of Loch Arkaig.

description of the Loch Arkaig lake horse or kelpie by a stalker and his boy.

The conspicuously whitewashed cottage at Murlaggan draws attention to itself, perhaps more so than in 1745 when the Jacobites used it for hiding French gold, not too far from Glenfinnan. Sgùrr Mhurlagain reaches 880m above it and, round the head of the loch are 858m Fraoch Bheinn, 1,040m Sgùrr na Ciche, 963m Sgùrr Thuilm, 909m Streap and 987m Gaor Bheinn, below which the Allt Camgharaidh enters the loch.

Hidden in the woods on the north side is the Allt Mhuic Butterfly Reserve.

Below 727m Mullach Coire nan Geur-oirean on the south side and 656m Meall Blair and 804m Geal Chàrn on the north

↑ Murlaggan below Sgùrr Mhurlagain.

↓ Gaor Bheinn from the mouth of the Allt Camgharaidh.

the loch reaches its greatest depth of more than 100m.

The east end of the loch is more wooded and the River Mallie joins below 771m Beinn Bhàn.

There is a fish farm at Achnasaul. Boats are often used by anglers.

As the loch narrows down there are a couple of islands, one with the remains of a chapel that must have had a limited congregation.

The loch ends as a bridge crosses with a rough weir beneath, the start of the 2km River Arkaig to Loch Lochy. Joining by the bridge is the Abhainn Chia-aig stream, which has waterfalls including the dramatic Eas Chia-aig by the road. Passing these falls is the Mile Dorcha, an avenue

↑ Looking up Glen Mallie from the Achnasaul fish farm.

↓ Chapel remains at Achnasaul hidden in trees on an island.

↓ The short River Arkaig leaves the loch at Achnacarry.

of beech trees, the setting for the finale of DK Broster's novel *The Dark Mile*.

Achnacarry House has been the seat of the Camerons of Locheil since 1660. The present building from 1802 has Gothic decoration, corner turrets and a crenellated parapet. This was the Commando Basic Training Centre during the Second World War, with 25,000 commandos having trained here. In 1928 the Achnacarry Agreement was an attempt to set petroleum production quotas, the Organization of the Petroleum Exporting Countries (OPEC) not being formed until 1960.

The Clan Cameron Museum in a 17th-century croft house pays special attention to armed forces.

DISTANCE_____
18km from Strathan to Achnacarry

OS 1:50,000 SHEETS_____
33 Loch Alsh, Glen Shiel & Loch Hourn
34 Fort Augustus, Glen Roy & Glen Moriston

→ Eas Chia-aig on the Abhainn Chia-aig.

LOCH LINNHE

FOLLOWING THE GREAT SLIP

21

Oh-hon, an righ! and the Stuarts of Appin!
The gallant, devoted, old Stuarts of Appin!
Their glory is o'er, for their star is no more,
And the green grass waves over the heroes of Appin!
JAMES HOGG

LOCH LINNHE

Loch Linnhe was previously thought to be a pre-glacial river that ran through the North Channel and Irish Sea with the Sound of Mull rift valley as a tributary. It is deep enough to be used as a submarine exercise area. Wind is funnelled along the loch and rainfall is increased. The peaks are shrouded in cloud, mist, rain or some other meteorological form more than 80% of the time.

The West Highland line follows the loch head from Corpach to Fort William.

It's a stunning route in its own right but the Jacobite steam train service adds further interest for railway and Harry Potter enthusiasts. The A830, built in 1812 by Telford, is the current Road to the Isles.

Corpach Light, a 6m white cylindrical tower with dark conical roof, marks the Sea Lock at the start of the Caledonian Canal, which gives boats an inland route north-east across Scotland to Inverness. Flows off Corpach are up to

↓ Ben Nevis rises above Loch Linnhe.

→ The Jacobite
arrives at Corpach.

↓ Corpach Sea
Lock on the
Caledonian Canal.

5km/h (3 knots), after which currents are much weaker.

Beyond Caol a peninsula separates the River Lochy at Inverlochy from Am Breun Chamas sands with the long island of An Caol running parallel. Otters and roe deer might be seen here.

The River Nevis also joins from south of the red and grey granite Ben Nevis, the highest mountain in Britain at 1,345m. Being 7km from the water makes its presence very obvious down Loch Eil to the west of Loch Linnhe at its northern end, although the summit is usually lost in cloud.

From the jetty at Camusnagaul a passenger ferry operates across to Fort William. The town was founded in 1654 by General Monck; most of the original site is now covered by the station. A stone fort replaced it in 1690 for William III to control the Highlanders. It was the main emigration port for Highlanders in the 19th century. Now it is a tourist centre, the capital of Lochaber, and full of hikers with rucksacks. A heliport and Underwater Centre are more functional. There is also a mountain rescue post. The West Highland Museum features the Jacobites, bagpipes recovered from Culloden, Celtic relics, arms, clans, tartans, archaeology, wildlife and an unusual 18th century portrait that looks like a blur until reflected in a polished

← The Cona Glen and Glen Scaddle lead into Inverscaddle Bay.

cylinder, when it reveals a portrait of Prince Charlie. There is also the Scottish Crafts & Whisky Centre.

The shores of Loch Linnhe run straight at first. Material has been washed into the loch at Stronchreggan by the Abhainn Sron a' Chreagain, but the River Kiachnish has made little impact on the east shore.

The River Scaddle empties into Inverscaddle Bay and gives views towards the peaks round the Cona Glen. The bay has Eilean nan Gall in the centre but drains at low water. It has the rare floating seaweed *Ascophyllum mackayii*, which has no roots and is unanchored, resting on the mud in mats when the tide is out.

Flows through the Corran Narrows are fast, officially to 9km/h (5 knots), although some say to 22km/h (12 knots)

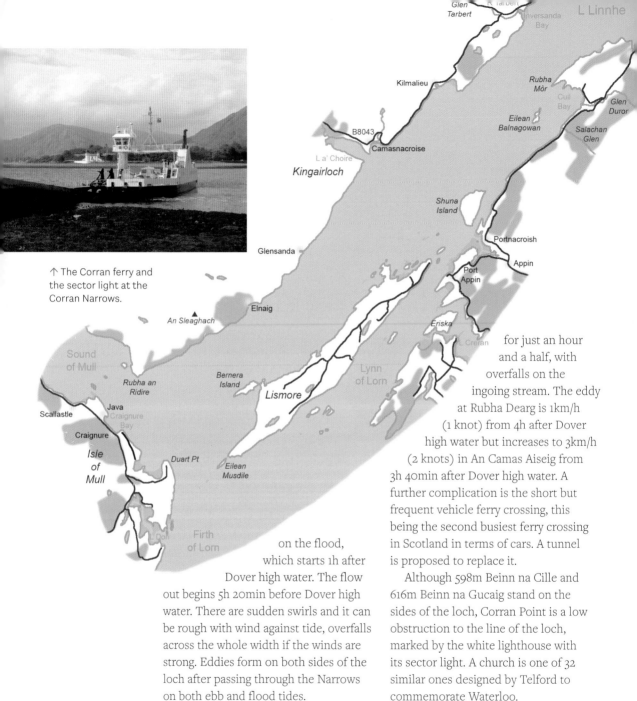

↑ The Corran ferry and the sector light at the Corran Narrows.

for just an hour and a half, with overfalls on the ingoing stream. The eddy at Rubha Dearg is 1km/h (1 knot) from 4h after Dover high water but increases to 3km/h (2 knots) in An Camas Aiseig from 3h 40min after Dover high water. A further complication is the short but frequent vehicle ferry crossing, this being the second busiest ferry crossing in Scotland in terms of cars. A tunnel is proposed to replace it.

Although 598m Beinn na Cille and 616m Beinn na Gucaig stand on the sides of the loch, Corran Point is a low obstruction to the line of the loch, marked by the white lighthouse with its sector light. A church is one of 32 similar ones designed by Telford to commemorate Waterloo.

The Abhainn Righ flows down from Glenrigh Forest past a forest trail and

on the flood, which starts 1h after Dover high water. The flow out begins 5h 20min before Dover high water. There are sudden swirls and it can be rough with wind against tide, overfalls across the whole width if the winds are strong. Eddies form on both sides of the loch after passing through the Narrows on both ebb and flood tides.

An Camas Aiseig has a south-easterly flow for eleven hours and north-westerly the shoreside Bunree Caravan Club Site. The water is clear, but there can be midges. Flows begin south-west 5h before Dover high water and north-east 1h 10min after Dover high water at up to 4km/h (2 knots) in the centre of the channel off Rubha Cuil-cheanna, the end of Loch Leven. At Onich there is the Clach-a-Charra standing stone site. The Ballachulish Bridge can be seen crossing the mouth of the loch with a backdrop of Glencoe peaks.

From Rubh' a' Bhaid Bheithe both sides of Loch Linnhe show precipitous mountains with steep valleys. Disused quarries are the toenails of 1,024m Sgòrr Dhearg.

A pier precedes Kentallen Bay, which appears sheltered except from the north but can produce violent squalls in various directions with westerly gales. Above is Glen Duror Forest.

Crom-Roinn is part of a low shoreline that initially has a park-like feel towards Rubha nam Mòine and remains low to Rubha Mòr, the outer point of Cuil Bay, which has been declared the best beach in Scotland in one survey. The River

Duror enters at the back of the bay.

The Salachan Burn enters opposite Eilean Balnagowan, an island with some sheltered inlets that have been declared a bird sanctuary and where porpoises might be seen.

Flows through the Sound of Shuna run south-west from 5h 40min before Dover high water and north-east from 40min after Dover high water at up to 2km/h (1 knot). The shelter by the

↑ The Ballachulish Bridge crosses the mouth of Loch Leven.

↓ Sgòrr Dhearg guards the end of Glen Duror.

→ Reefs are marked to the north of Port Appin. Beyond are Shuna Island and the Kingairloch mountains.

Knap encourages its use for moorings. There is also a fish farm near the ruins of the small square Castle Shuna. The flat-topped island is a single farm.

In the centre of Loch Laich on the eastern side is Castle Stalker. From about 1500 it was the seat of the Stewarts of Appin before becoming the 16th century hunting lodge of James IV. In *Monty Python & the Holy Grail* it was used as Castle Aargh!

Eilean nan Caorach with its limekilns, Inn Island and Sgeir Bhuidhe with its 8m white tower produce the Appin Narrows, flowing south-west as at the Sound of Shuna and north-east from 30min after Dover high water at up to 5km/h (3 knots).

From Port Appin, a passenger ferry serves Lismore. This large island of Dalradian limestone is very fertile, hence its Gaelic name of Lios Mòr,

great garden. Most houses are towards the northern end.

At the far end of the outcrop is a natural arch overlooking Rubha Clach Tholl. Off this point are Appin Rocks across which both streams set strongly.

The channel widens out into the Lynn of Lorn in front of Airds Bay.

Loch Creran empties swiftly past Dearg Sgeir, Glas Eilean and the much larger Eriska, which is only an island when there is water in An Doirlinn.

↓ Castle Stalker in Loch Laich.

↑ Port Appin, the terminal for the passenger ferry to the Isle of Lismore.

A 5.5m iron cage marks Branra Rock, which has an artificial reef of concrete blocks on its west side, built for research by the Scottish Association for Marine Science. Eilean Dubh in the centre of the channel has heather on top and bootlace weed and anemones in the surrounding shallows. Flows run south-west from 5h 20min after Dover high water and north-east from 40min before Dover high water at up to 2km/h (1 knot).

From any distance the Kingairloch shore looks like a wall of mountains. In fact, they are not cliffs, but the peaks do rise quickly from behind the frequent stone beaches, most of which are inaccessible from landward.

Flows are up to 4km/h (2 knots) past Sallachan Point, marked by a red-painted octagonal beacon with a ball on top, and a boulder beach that reaches round into Camas Shallachain, another bay with a clockwise eddy during the ebb. Entering to the west of the aerial past Sallachan is the River Gour, which drains down from

↑ A natural arch by Appin Rocks.

← An otter with fish near Branra Rock. Beyond is Lismore.

↓ Mountains around Loch Creran lie to the east.

↑ Glen Gour, looking towards Beinn na h-Uamha.

the Ardgour mountains.

The peaks now close in with 508m Beinn Leamhain only 1km from the shore, and rising beyond to 650m Sgòrr Mhic Eacharna and 885m Garbh Bheinn. At Inversanda Bay the River Tarbert discharges into a sheltered inlet.

The 509m Meall a' Bhràghaid starts the Kingairloch proper, the first 6km with no road, just rocks covered with barnacles and limpets. The Sgeirean nan Torran are only small islets but prove useful landmarks halfway down this section of remote shore.

Rubha na h-Earba introduces Camas Chìl Mhalieu and an eddy that works on the flood for 6km to beyond the

mouth of Loch a' Choire. The B8043 follows the shore at the back of the eddy to Rubha na h-Àirde Uinnsinn, after which the coast is largely remote from roads to the Sound of Mull.

Camas na Croise receives the Glengalmadale River, which descends between 591m Meall nan Each and 651m Beinn na Cille. Loch a' Choire with its large fish farm not only receives water from the Abhainn na Coinnich but also violent squalls that rush down off the mountains. A couple of aerials are located by the road as it turns inland past the prominent 739m Beinn Mheadhoin.

The ebb begins 5h before Dover high water and the flood 1h 20min after Dover

↓ Glen Tarbert runs down to Inversanda Bay.

↑ Approaching Inversanda Bay with Torr an Fhamhair.

high water at up to 1km/h (1 knot), taking with it moon and lion's mane jellyfish and Atlantic grey seals.

Between 569m Sgurr a'Bhuic and 474m Meall na h-Easaiche, a pair of streams dropping down Dearg Uillt have blasted through the bank of stones that form the shoreline. It is possible to sit at the bottom and look up the lines of these kilometre-long streams falling down straight courses at a 50% gradient.

Round the corner the red granite is being removed fast from Glensanda Harbour where a jetty with a moving conveyor loads crushed granite on to 150,000-tonne bulk carriers. This is Aggregate Industries' 1980s super quarry, the first in Britain and the largest granite quarry in Europe. It has a visual impact greater than had been anticipated by the planning authorities. Each of the buttresses left on the front face is larger than the cube of the nearby castle, built in the 15th century by Ewen MacLean.

There is an hour and a half stand at high water with flows to 2km/h (1 knot). In the Lynn of Morvern the ebb begins 5h before high water at Dover to 2km/h (1 knot), but the flood starts 1h 20min after Dover high water to 6km/h (3 knots), setting towards Sgeir nan Tom to the north of Lismore. Winds are unpredictable but usually parallel to the coast.

The wall of peaks continues. Below them is Eignaig, a settlement of three buildings.

The main water activity takes place off Rubha a'Mhòthair. On springs, overfalls reach from 200m east of the point nearly to Rubha Croinn on Bernera Island from the start of the ebb for three to four hours, the edge of the overfalls being sharply defined at the northern end. The ebb flow causes eddies and further interest was added by using this as an explosives dumping ground in the past.

Rubha an Ridire with its basaltic cliffs is another interesting spot with strong tidal streams and eddies, races and heavy

→ Stranded moon jellyfish at Eignaig.

overfalls dangerous to small vessels with opposing wind. Flows from Loch Linnhe and the Sound of Mull meet here or divide according to the state of the tide. Flows begin north-west from 1h 20 mins after Dover high water to 6km/h (3 knots) and south-east from 5h 40min before high water at Dover to 4km/h (2 knots). A south-westerly wind can funnel along the sound from the Salen gap, while a north-easterly wind goes in the opposite direction.

Just beyond the point is Eilean Rubha an Ridire, an island coated with wrack at sea level and screaming with terns above. It has two wrecks on it, the northern one a historic vessel, 60m north of the point, with a 75m exclusion zone around it.

With suitable visibility the views are breathtaking, landmarks including the lighthouse on Eilean Musdile. A light marks the Glas Eileanan or grey rocks in the middle of the sound with flows to 3km/h (2 knots) as car ferries pass from Oban to Castlebay, Lochboisdale, Arinagour and Scarinish. There can be overfalls off Scallastle Point with Sgeir Mhic Chomhain and Sgeir nan Gobhar and to Loch Don. Beyond lies the Isle of Mull.

↓ Looking from Eignaig towards the Isle of Mull.

DISTANCE
73km from Kinlocheil to Eilean Dubh

OS 1:50,000 SHEETS
40 Mallaig & Glenfinnan
41 Ben Nevis, Fort William & Glen Coe
49 Oban & East Mull

TIDAL CONSTANTS
L Eil Head: Dover −0440
Corpach: HW Dover −0510,
LW Dover −0500
Corran: HW Dover −0510,
LW Dover −0520
Port Appin: HW Dover −0520,
LW Dover −0540
Craignure: HW Dover −0500,
LW Dover −0510

SEA AREA
Malin

RESCUE
Inshore lifeboats: Loch Ness,
Loch Lomond
All weather lifeboat: Oban

LOCH SUNART

DIAMONDS AND RED FLARES

22

Rising on Garbh Bheinn, the Carnoch River flows westwards down Glen Tarbert, becoming tidal from the A884. Gravel and cobble rapids lead down to Loch Sunart, which drains for the first 600m. It has knotted wrack, which is unrooted and unanchored, resting on the mud at the head of the loch when the tide is low. The loch, one of the most picturesque, runs west to the Sound of Mull and is a submarine exercise area. In earlier years it had a prolific herring fishing industry. Violent squalls can accompany easterly winds here.

The north shore is followed by the A861, engineered by Telford. Both sides of the loch are wooded extensively. On the north side the natural woods of oak, hazel and pine support lichens and are inhabited by badgers, pine martens, red squirrels, redstarts and long-tailed tits. In the water are salmon and sea trout. The colder south side has birches.

A slipway and jetty serve the north shore. Beyond a war memorial the Strontian River joins, emerging from woods filled with forests walks and a nature trail.

Strontian takes its name from Sròn an-t Sìthein, point of the fairies. It is where Frank Fraser Darling wrote

↑ Moorings off the war memorial at Strontian.

← Sgùrr Dhomhnuill faces the head of the loch.

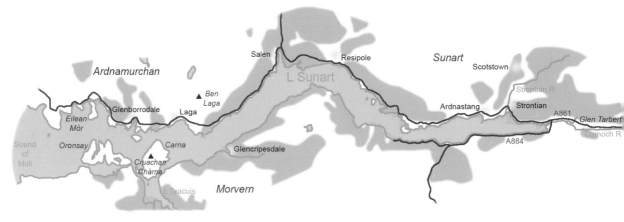

his *Natural History in the Highlands & Islands* and where author Gavin Maxwell discussed basking shark fishing with him. The prominent Strontian Hotel dates from the 18th century and used to be a hunting lodge.

The village has affluent residences as a result of prosperity from nearby mining. Lead, silver and zinc mines, up the valley at Scotstown, were used from 1722 to 1904. French prisoners of war discovered strontianite in 1790. Humphry Davy isolated the rare earth element strontium

from it in 1808 and for many years this was used to produce the crimson colour in flares and fireworks. Later, the radioisotopes strontium-89 and strontium-90 were discovered as by-products of nuclear fission.

Strontian has a Telford church but at Ardnastang, beyond Eilean a' Mhuirich, there used to be a boat moored at the jetty as a floating church because the estate owners refused a plot of land for a Free Church in the mid-19th century. They later relented and a redundant

↓ Rubha an Daimh on the north side of the loch.

church stands near the start of the old coffin route to the 16th century St Finan's Chapel on Eilean Fhianain in Loch Shiel.

A mussel farm on the south side precedes the Laudale Narrows, where Eilean Mór constricts the loch and produces flows up to 6km/h (3 knots). Small craft may be able to cut inside the island. Beyond the attractive wooded Rubha an Daimh are Garbh Eilean, Eilean a' Chuilinn and a bar running south-west across the loch. There is a forest walk and a hide with telescopes to train on wildlife, ranging from seals to eagles and herons. The land rises behind to the 845m-high Beinn Resipol.

Resipole is rather tame by comparison, with a golf course and campsite.

Limpets and barnacles adhere to lava rolls on the south shore around Rubha Aird Earnaich, behind which the land rises to 340m Gearr Chreag.

There are moorings around Salen Bay, a cleft in the north shore with Salen at its head, where Sunart gives way to Ardnamurchan. Weak flows are outgoing from 4h before Dover high water to 2h after Dover high water.

A barge jetty stands at the mouth of the Glencripesdale Burn, which flows down through Scottish Natural Heritage's Glencripesdale Nature Reserve. It is visited by sea eagles and reaches nearly to the 571m summit of Beinn Iadain.

At the foot of 512m Ben Laga, a drying reef connected to the shore was chosen as the site for Dùn Ghallain. A jetty in Laga Bay serves Laga.

The rugged island of Carna, formerly populated, rises to the 169m peak of

↑ The channel
between the north
side of the loch and
the island of Risga.

Finding a route inside Eilean an Fhèidh is more difficult. This is a breeding area for terns, oystercatchers, eider ducks and mergansers.

Around Glenborrodale is the eponymous hamlet. There is a conspicuous modern house by the water. Most significant is the 1900 Victorian castle in red Annan sandstone, built for Charles Rudd, partner of Cecil Rhodes in the De Beers Diamond Corporation. His second wife refused to live in it and, in 1969, it became a hotel. The coach house and stables are centuries old, for a much earlier building.

Glenborrodale has ancient oak wood with nesting wood warblers and many other woodland birds. It is an RSPB reserve. At the head of Glenmore Bay is the Ardnamurchan Natural History Visitor Centre.

The low, barren, rocky island of Oronsay, almost connected to the southern shore, was formerly populated.

Cruachan Chàrna. Each side of it is a narrow passage to Loch Teacuis, which cuts deep into the Morvern peninsula. Carna also obstructs the south side of Loch Sunart, although small craft find a channel to the north of Risga with its cup-marked rocks. Flows are as at Salen but only up to 5km/h (3 knots).

It is so divided by north–south inlets that it is almost three islands.

Eilean Mòr on the north side of Loch Sunart is connected to the shore by a drying reef, except at the top of spring tides. Rubha Aird Shlignich forms the northern gatepost to the loch. Flows north-west out of the loch run from 4h 50min before Dover high water and north-east into the loch from 10min before Dover high water at up to 2km/h (1 knot).

Outside the loch, 528m Ben Hiant faces Mull and the Sound of Mull.

DISTANCE
20km from Carnoch to Oronsay

OS 1:50,000 SHEETS
40 Mallaig & Glenfinnan
47 Tobermory & North Mull
49 Oban & East Mull

TIDAL CONSTANTS
Salen: HW Dover –0520,
LW Dover –0510
Tobermory: HW Dover –0500

SEA AREA
Malin

RESCUE
Inshore lifeboat: Kyle of Lochalsh
All weather lifeboat: Tobermory

↑ The castle in red sandstone at Glenborrodale.

23

LOCH SHIEL

THE START OF THE 45 REBELLION

LOCH SHIEL

And see a small devoted band,
By dark Loch Shiel have ta'en their stand.
And proudly vow with heart and hand,
To fight for Royal Charlie.
AGNES MAXWELL MACLEOD

Glenfinnan is bounded by high peaks,
notably 790m Fraoch Bheinn and 810m
Beinn an Tuim, the haunt of birds of
prey that may be seen wheeling above
the mountainsides.

The most dramatic structure is
the 380m-long curved mass concrete
Glenfinnan Viaduct of 1901, which
consists of 21 semi-circular arches up to
30m high. It carries the West Highland
railway line, renowned for its dramatic
scenery and probably the most beautiful
line in Britain. Trains have included
observation cars and steam trains are
being run in the summer, now with added
interest because of its use in the Harry
Potter films, the loch itself serving as the

→ The Glenfinnan
Monument marks
the spot at the head
of Loch Shiel where
Prince Charlie raised
the Stuart standard
to start the '45
Rebellion.

Great Lake at Hogwarts School.

The River Finnan is finally tamed beyond the A830. On the southern side of the road and the west bank of the river is a small car park that suffers from midges in season. The car park on the other side of the river at the information centre has the benefit of public toilets. The information is on the 1815 Glenfinnan Monument, which stands by the head of Loch Shiel, marking the spot where Prince Charlie raised the Stuart standard and gathered 1,500 clansmen on 19 August 1745 to begin the '45 Rebellion, the second Jacobite uprising.

Ahead stretches Loch Shiel, running almost dead straight for 18km before going into a series of kinks at its southern end. The Callop River enters on the south side past the memorial column and the Abhainn Shlatach balances it on the other side after the pier at Glenfinnan. A few boats are moored, giving access to the fish farm tanks just beyond on the northern side.

↑ A train passes over the Glenfinnan Viaduct.

↓ The head of Loch Shiel, seen from Glenfinnan Viaduct.

↑ Looking down the long, unbroken straight that is Loch Shiel.

The mountains are grand in the extreme, sloping down with almost unbroken gradient into the water. Beinn Odhar Mhòr of 870m and the higher 882m Beinn Odhar Bheag on the north-west side are the highest, but some of the peaks forming the south bank have more character, especially 634m Meall a' Choire Chruinn and the corrie itself with the Allt Coire Ghiùbhsachain emerging in a series of falls from behind a prominent ridge. The mountains suggest only a small trough of water lies between them, but that trough reaches a depth of more than 120m.

The loch is oligotrophic, that is, relatively poor in plant nutrients and containing abundant oxygen in the deeper parts. Those lines of peaks funnel the prevailing south-westerly wind in an effective wind tunnel for which the only consolation is that the largest waves are met first of all. Even if the wind is from another direction it should be remembered that wind, clouds and weather can change with startling rapidity here and that individual peaks can produce dramatic local variations, particularly in wind direction.

Where there are trees on the north-west shore they are mostly oaks, whereas the other side has been planted with firs in places. This latter side is accessible from a track that runs along the shore of the loch.

Halfway along the first reach the

Glenaladale River enters from the north, opposite the small community of Scamodale. The naturist beach at its mouth must be one of the least accessible in the country.

Little by little the mountains reduce in height towards the south-west, the exception being the huge rounded bulk of 845m Beinn Resipol to the south. The River Polloch enters from the southern side just before the loch goes into the first of two S bends. The second reduces the dividing line between Moidart to the north and Sunart to the south to less than 200m width before the loch turns due west, widens and then begins to taper down again. It immediately passes Eilean Fhianain, which has several gravestones visible and is the site of St Finnan's Chapel.

Fish farms begin to appear again, together with moored boats, notably at Dalelia.

The south side is no longer mountainous, at least in the foreground.

DISTANCE_____
27km from Glenfinnan to Acharacle

OS 1:50,000 SHEET_____
40 Mallaig & Glenfinnan

Instead, Claish Moss stretches for several kilometres, a raised bog that is a notable wildlife reserve.

Gradually, housing begins to appear at Langal, Dalnabreck and Mingarry Park on the north shore. At first the south side is undeveloped with just the occasional stunted tree breaking the shoreline, but when these give way to lifebelts it is clear that civilization is being approached. This is duly reached with Ardshealach and Acharacle and their numerous boats.

Passing a large disused boathouse at Claish Moss together with a shoreline of rhododendrons and gorse, the loch finally slims down yet further and picks up speed as the River Shiel takes over.

↓ Claish Moss is a raised peat bog that acts as an important wildlife reserve. Left is Beinn Resipol.

24 LOCH MORAR

SINGULARLY INACCESSIBLE

LOCH MORAR

His Leagsaidh, born while he was with his sheep,
Baptized in Morar, twenty miles away,
Spent childhood in this almost empty glen.
JOHN HARGREAVES

Kinlochmorar is a singularly inaccessible place. The nearest road is 12km away as the crow flies, at the head of Loch Arkaig. The only lochside road is on the north side at the western end, but it reaches only to Bracorina and there is nowhere to leave a vehicle. The best place is where the river leaves the loch and to undertake an out and back trip.

At the head of the loch is 589m Meall nan Each, rising to 829m Carn Mór. Several ruined buildings remain at Kinlochmorar, from where the route on the water lies due west.

Loch Morar is more sheltered than

the sea lochs but can still be subject to sudden storms. Mountain heights decline westwards.

There are occasional oak or birch woods, but the vegetation is mostly heather with some bracken. There are sheep, buzzards, herons and greylag geese might be seen and the cuckoo heard. There are shingle beaches in places and nobody is likely to be using them.

Gleann Taodhail joins before the Druim a' Chùirn shoulder runs along the south side of the loch up to 584m.

Sgùrr Mòr, at 612m, sees the ridge on the north side starting to drop down

↓ Meall nan Each and An Stac at the head of Loch Morar.

Mallaig
Morar
Bracorina
L Nevis
Tarbet
Swordland
Kinlochmorar
Carn Mór
L Morar
Oban
R Meoble
An Stac
Meoble

↓ The Druim a' Chùirn shoulder on the south side of Loch Morar.

towards South Tarbet Bay. A portage route from Tarbet on Loch Nevis comes over the ridge and drops down to South Tarbet Bay or branches off on a slightly longer and less steep route to Swordland. The portage is described in JL Henderson's 1951 book, *Kayak to Cape Wrath*. Although used occasionally, it is no easy stroll, as a glance at the terrain will indicate.

Off Swordland is the deepest fresh water in Britain, at 310m. This is the result of tectonic movement. The abyssal temperature is 6°C and, of course, it has a monster, Morag, usually only seen when

↑ The central part of the loch.

→ Swordland at the start of a less than easy portage.

↑ Leac Bhuidhe with Druim Ile Coire on the right.

the death of a MacDonald of Clanranald is expected. In 1969 a man appeared on television with a damaged oar, which he claimed Morag had chomped. Far from being terrified, he seemed rather sheepish so perhaps other water users should be equally unconcerned about being attacked by the monster.

Between Camas Luinge and the River Meoble there is a pier that serves the isolated hamlet of Meoble. French commandos were trained at Meoble

← Wooded shoreline at Brinacory.

↑ Looking south past Brinacory Island.

Lodge by the Special Operations Executive during the Second World War, while Belgian commandos were trained from Rhubana Lodge at the western end of the loch.

↑ Boat moorings at the start of the River Morar.

→ Skeletal tree at Loch Morar.

Brinacory Island is wooded, as is the adjacent shoreline.

Ungrazed pine islands stand across the loch as it shallows at its western end, including Eilean a' Phidhir, Eilean nam Breac, An t-Eilean Meadhoin and Eilean Bàn. Simon Fraser, the chief of the Fraser clan at the time, was perhaps unwise in openly declaring his support for Prince Charlie. After Culloden he used one of these islands to hide. Some sailors from a warship moored in Morar Bay happened to land here and found him in a hollow tree. He was sent to London where he had the dubious distinction of being the last person in England to be beheaded with an axe.

The loch, still with clear water, feeds into the River Morar past a church, cemetery and moorings for motorboats at Morar.

DISTANCE
18km from Kinlochmorar to Morar

OS 1:50,000 SHEET
40 Mallaig & Glenfinnan

↑ Looking east past the islands to the peaks of Morar.

LOCH NEVIS

The River Carnach feeds into Loch Nevis, one of the most beautiful sea lochs. It is tidal from below Carnoch, cutting through peat and over small stone rapids, home to dragonflies and red deer. The head of the loch drains for a kilometre past the peninsula of Eilean Tioram to Eilean Maol, which is covered with bracken and heather. The intertidal sand and stones upstream also extend eastwards to Sourlies, said to be the loneliest house in Scotland.

At the head of the loch are the 1,040m pyramid of Sgùrr na Cìche, breast peak, and 1,013m Garbh Chioch Mhòr. The Knoydart peaks of Meall Bhasiter at 718m and 855m Beinn Bhuidhe, yellow hill, face

→ A red deer stag watches the river at Carnoch.

↓ A track leads away from Tarbet to Loch Morar.

859m Sgurr na h-Aide, 747m Sgurr nam Meirleach, 728m Sgùrr Breac and 612m Sgùrr Mòr, which separate the loch from Loch Morar, which lies parallel. A pier at Torr Cruinn is used for moorings for the head of the loch.

Loch Nevis is 146m deep off 522m Sgurr an Eilein Ghiubhais; it also reaches 101m depth above Kylesknoydart.

Although sheltered from the north by the Knoydart mountains, the loch is subject to violent squalls that can be dangerous to small boats. These can come from various directions but are worst from the east.

↓ Seals resting west of the narrows.

Creag Chruachain overshadows Kylesknoydart and Kylesmorar, narrow and relatively shallow with a large drying area of stones at Roinn á Chaolais on the west side. Although flows of the clear water are generally imperceptible in the loch, they can reach 6km/h (3 knots) through the narrows.

From Tarbet Bay a track winds up over the pass to Loch Morar; this is sometimes used as a portage trail. Tarbet is served by passenger ferry from Mallaig via Inverie. The chapel there has been converted to a bothy. Despite the risk of squalls with south-westerly winds, this was the main fishing village on the loch and used to have a prolific herring fishing industry until the railway came to Mallaig. Today there are mackerel and saithe.

Ardintigh Point contains Ardintigh Bay, as Torr nan Gamhainn contains Stoul. North of Port Longaig the loch reaches the limit of Mallaig Harbour control. There are fish farms on the west side and porpoises sport in the loch.

Behind 395m A' Chruach the Inverie River enters Inverie Bay, backed by 796m Sgùrr Coire Choinnichean and 441m Roinn ne Beinn. A forested area stands above Inverie, a former fishing community and the capital of Knoydart, with a memorial. A road runs from here through Scottas but only as far as Airor so it acts as an island as far as vehicles are concerned. The Old Forge is claimed to be the most remote pub in mainland Britain, 29km on foot from Kinloch Hourn or effectively a 10km sea crossing from Mallaig.

A waterfall drops from Glaschoille Loch, in front of which are the Sgeirean Glasa with a metal tripod beacon. Norwegian commandos were trained from Glaschoille House by the Special Operations Executive during the Second World War. Rubha Raonuill has a couple of caves and another mark, but the

← A porpoise hunting near the mouth of the loch.

distinctive feature is a white statue of the Virgin Mary.

Flows start out of the loch 5h 20min before Dover high water and return from 1h after Dover high water at up to 1km/h (1 knot). South-easterly and south-westerly winds are the worst in this area. Ahead is the Sound of Sleat with Skye's low Sleat Peninsula, the peaks of the Black Cuillin rising beyond.

← The Virgin Mary statue stands out clearly on Rubha Raonuill.

DISTANCE
16km from Carnoch to Sgurr an Eilean Ghiubhais

OS 1:50,000 SHEETS
33 Loch Alsh, Glen Shiel & Loch Hourn (40 Mallaig & Glenfinnan)

TIDAL CONSTANTS
Inverie Bay: HW Dover −0500, LW Dover −0450

SEA AREA
Hebrides

RESCUE
Inshore lifeboat: Kyle of Lochalsh
All weather lifeboat: Mallaig

26 LOCH HOURN

DARK, BEAUTIFUL AND REMOTE

LOCH HOURN

This is Scotland's most remote western sea loch. Kinloch Hourn is reached along a 35km dead-end single lane road where red deer might lie on the verge or highland cattle settle down on the carriageway. The final part is very steep and twisting.

It is joined by the Allt Coire Sgoireadail, which flows south-west to Loch Beag, the initial part of Loch Hourn.

The first 400m of the loch drains with the tide.

One of Scotland's most spectacular lochs, Loch Hourn has been glaciated, but the first half, sometimes known as Loch Hourn Beag, is narrow. It is frequently referred to as dark Loch Hourn, the name meaning hell, and is a good place to view the night sky. This is partly because Knoydart's high

↓ Sgùrr a' Mhaoraich overlooks the head of Loch Hourn.

↓ Loch Beag with Carn nan Caorach and the Fourth Narrows.

mountains block out sunlight from the south but also because of the weather. It has one of the highest rainfalls in Britain and there is often low cloud.

There can be strong winds from the south and west. Violent squalls from high ground have unpredictable direction. Facing the head of the loch is 1,027m Sgùrr a' Mhaoraich at the west end of Glenquoich Forest. The roaring of red deer provides sounds that can vary from

a noise like cattle to downright eerie as they bellow across the loch.

Flows are outgoing from 4h 20min before Dover high water and ingoing from 1h 50min after Dover high water, with strong flows through the narrows. The Fourth Narrows are near the head of the loch.

Raptors include golden eagles, herons are frequent and there are cormorants. The north side of the loch is wooded, initially followed by power lines, while the south side is followed by a footpath skirting the feet of 738m Sgùrr Dubh and 881m Sgùrr Sgiath-Airigh. From time to

↑ Caolasmòr obstructs the Second Narrows.

↑ Coir' a' Chearcaill towers above Barrisdale Bay.

time it passes a stone building, such as the abandoned one at Skiary by the most sheltered part of the loch.

Eilean Mhogh-sgeir sits in the centre of the Third Narrows and Caolasmòr passes the Second Narrows. Meall nan Eun at 666m and Carn Màiri at 502m shade the south side and Druim Fada descending from 713m is to the north of the First Narrows. Here, flows can be 6km/h (3 knots), especially on the north side, although there is an outgoing eddy on the south side during the flood. Fraoch Eilean, Eilean Choinnich and Eilean a' Gharb-làin contribute to the

constriction, with the Corr Eileanan forming another line out from A' Chiste Dhubh.

From here the loch is wider. The River Barrisdale empties sand into Barrisdale Bay, but the loch then becomes much deeper and is able to take large vessels. Above the bay is an impressive corrie with a rock wall on its west side and a conical peak above. Ladhar Bheinn is 1,020m high, its peak only 3km from the shore. At its foot is Eilean a' Mhuineil, which closes in Poll a' Mhuineil but does not block the fierce squalls that can arrive in bad weather.

There are shielings above Eilean a' Phiobaire on the south side before Rubha Ruadh and a fish farm. Rubha Camas na Cailinn on the opposite shore is followed by Sgeir Leathan and then by Corran where the River Arnisdale joins at Crudha Àrd. This is the road head, but the road journey from Kinloch Hourn is more than 100km longer than the distance on the water.

At Arnisdale, Camas Bàn, sheltered by Eilean Tioram, has another fish farm. Behind the village, Beinn Bhuidhe leads into a great unbroken ridge that runs to 974m Beinn Sgritheall, its summit only 1.6km from the shore. Along its foot are the Sgeirean Ràrsaidh. Caolas Eilean Ràrsaidh runs inside Eilean a' Chuilinn and Eilean Ràrsaidh.

The approach to Creag an t-Sagairt gives views straight across Skye's low Sleat Peninsula to the Cuillin Hills rising dramatically beyond. Off Rubha an Daraich is Sgeir Ulibhe with the remains of a metal day mark in the middle of the loch.

Beyond the stone building at Croulin the Croulin Burn discharges silt and is forming a spit. The Sound of Sleat is a submarine exercise area and is also used by basking sharks.

↑ Beinn Sgritheall dominates the lower half of the loch.

DISTANCE
18km from Kinloch Hourn to Croulin

OS 1:50,000 SHEET
33 Loch Alsh, Glen Shiel & Loch Hourn

TIDAL CONSTANTS
Loch Hourn: HW Dover −0520, LW Dover −0500

SEA AREA
Hebrides

RESCUE
All weather lifeboat: Mallaig

← The Cuillin Hills seen across Sleat from Creag an t-Sagairt.

27

LOCH DUICH

ONE OF SCOTLAND'S MOST PHOTOGRAPHED CASTLES

LOCH DUICH

Come up by Glen Duich, and doon by Glen Shee
An' roun' by Kinclaven and hither tae me,
For Ranald and Donald are oot on the fen,
Tae brak the wing o' my bonnie moorhen.
ANON

Ratagan has several advantages as a launch point for portable boats onto Loch Duich. The village is quiet, parking is no problem and there is easy access from a lawn area, avoiding most of the drying area that stretches out for up to 700m at the head of the loch. There is an SYHA youth hostel beside the loch.

Not least are the spectacular views. To the south-east the Five Sisters of Kintail stand above Glen Shiel, while, to the north-east, 918m A' Ghlas-bheinn is between the peaks of Kintail Forest and Inverinate Forest, the mountains steep and sharp. The River Shiel arrives between 876m Sgùrr na Mòraich and 779m Sgùrr Mhic Bharraich.

The shores of the loch are also steep, partially wooded with firs that are being forested, as the loch reaches north-west without deviation to join Loch Alsh.

Ratagan has declined in importance. The minor road along the south-west shore used to be the main road north-west, although the route to Skye, as used

↓ A' Ghlas-bheinn above the north-eastern corner of Loch Duich.

← Sgùrr an Airgid above Inverinate.

L Long
Dornie
L Alsh
Totaig
Inverinate ▲
Sgurr an Airgid
Beinn a' Chuirn
L Duich
A87
Ratagan
Shiel Bridge
Kintail Forest
5 Sisters
R Shiel
Sgurr Mhic Bharraich
Glen Shiel

by Johnson and Boswell, was over the 340m Mam Ratagan Pass, the approach running just above the village.

The switchover to the north-east shore, as used by the A87, came after Telford built the crossing at Shiel Bridge in 1820. The initial route 200m above the loch is now a scenic route, having been succeeded by the road that runs along or near the shore.

For early visitors attempting the north-east side of the loch, Dùnan Diarmid was sited at the mouth of the River Cree.

The River Shiel discharges into the loch over a bed of small boulders between shallows covered in wrack. Jellyfish in the water include lion's mane specimens.

Inverinate is below 941m Sgùrr an Airgid. The An Leth-allt falls to the loch opposite 603m Beinn a' Chuirn, below which are a jetty, a dun and a fish farm.

The loch runs straight to meet Loch Alsh and towards the mountain wall that extends from Beinn Conchra. Guarding the three-way junction between Loch Duich, Loch Long and Loch Alsh is Eilean Donan Castle.

Eilean Donan is one of the most photographed castles in Scotland. A three-arched bridge of 1912 crosses a drying reef and feeds through the portcullis of the ivy-covered castle on St Donan's isle.

Colin Fitzgerald, the son of Earl Desmond, was given land by Alexander III to build a castle to resist the Danes. He had it built in 1230 on the site of

↓ The Five Sisters of Kintail at the head of the loch.

↑ Eilean Donan Castle stands at the entrance to Loch Duich.

an earlier fort. After its capture for the king by the Earl of Huntly it became the ancestral home of the MacKenzies of Kintail. It was destroyed in 1719 by three Royal Navy frigates while being held for the Old Pretender by the Spanish.

Refurbishment was undertaken from 1912 to 1932 by Colonel MacRae, the MacRaes having been hereditary constables of the MacKenzies since the 16th century. The Billeting Room walls are up to 4.3m thick. Furnishing is in medieval style with MacRae portraits. The castle was used for filming *Highlander* and *Loch Ness* and it was the Scottish headquarters of MI6 in the James Bond film, *The World is Not Enough*.

Eilean Tioram, in the centre of the loch, is low and grassy, but Totaig is steep and rugged. A slipway for a former passenger ferry from Totaig across the

end of Loch Duich precedes a sheltered mooring behind a small island, an inlet across the mouth of which the water boils and swirls. Herons stand among the kelp.

Eilean Aoinidh, where Loch Duich joins Loch Alsh, is not an island.

DISTANCE
9km from Shiel Bridge to Totaig

OS 1:50,000 SHEET
(25 Glen Carron & Glen Affric)
33 Loch Alsh, Glen Shiel & Loch Hourn

TIDAL CONSTANTS
Dornie Bridge: HW Dover −0440,
LW Dover −0430

SEA AREA
Hebrides

RESCUE
Inshore lifeboat: Kyle of Lochalsh
All weather lifeboats: Mallaig, Portree

LOCH ALSH

IMPORTANT RECENT BRIDGES

28

LOCH ALSH

Trees cloak the south shore of Loch Alsh round into Kyle Rhea, hiding the Caisteal Grugaig broch, an Iron Age Pictish fort. A huge triangular block above the door, wall chambers and parts of a staircase and gallery remain.

There are extensive shallows off Ardelve and in Nostie Bay, while Glas Eilean is flat and green, as its name claims. The only break in the trees on the south shore is around Ardintoul, where the point is low and cultivated. Beyond Kyle Rhea is Skye, dominated at this end by the 739m rounded bulk of Sgùrr na Coinnich. Flows along the south side of the loch are to 2km/h (1 knot), the west-going stream increased in strength and duration by snow melt, heavy rain and southerly or south-westerly winds. Meanwhile, the east-going stream is reduced correspondingly, while northerly winds have the opposite effect.

Points each side of Avenish are rocky, covered with barnacles and limpets, as is the foot of Aird Hill, itself at the foot of 344m Sgùrr Mòr, a peak covered with trees and heather. Sea urchins, starfish and scallop shells may be seen in the water.

Balmacara Bay can have a short sea with southerly or south-westerly winds. A war memorial and a cemetery face the bay, as does the Lochalsh Woodland

↓ Glas Bheinn and Sgùrr na Coinnich stand above Kyle Rhea with Knoydart peaks to the south.

↑ Sgùrr na Coinnich on Skye at the far end of the loch with the Cuillin peaks beyond.

Kyle Akin takes its name from King Haakon IV of Norway, who sailed through in 1263 prior to his defeat at the Battle of Largs. The Eileanan Dubha, at the east end of the kyle, are covered with heather and have a light on a 5m white metal framework.

Rubha Àrd Treisnis, at the mouth of Loch na Bèiste, is followed by Caisteal Maol, built for Danish princess 'Saucy Mary', who stretched a chain across the kyle to collect tolls from passing ships. It was a MacKinnon stronghold from the 12th to 15th centuries.

The slipway was the main access point for Skye before the bridge was built, connecting with Kyle of Lochalsh despite the fast flows through the kyle. Kyleakin was a fishing port before becoming a ferry terminal. On the sides of the mouth of An t-Ob, there is a war memorial and the Bright Water Visitor Centre.

Kyle of Lochalsh expanded after the arrival of the railway from Inverness in 1897, its platform formerly used for council meetings and the refreshment room serving drinks long after trains

Garden of 1887, with gardens, terraces, woodland natural coastline and a visitor centre in a coach house, all part of the Balmacara Estate.

Beyond a ruined jetty is an 8m white granite monument to Colonel Donald Murchison, tax collector for the exiled Jacobite 5th Earl of Seaforth, a hazardous occupation that won him a spell in the Tower of London before being pardoned and given land by George I.

had departed for the night. These days the station buildings have been partly converted to Kyle Railway Museum and the Waterside Seafood Restaurant, visiting drivers doing three-point turns on the station platform. The Lochalsh Hotel is prominent, but the inshore lifeboat has to be towed down the road from its building hidden near the station.

Replacing the ferry is the Skye Bridge of 1996, originally notorious for its high toll but now toll free. The balanced cantilever concrete box structure takes the A87 over an arch high enough to clear shipping. At its northern end is Eilean Bàn, white island, with Stevenson's Kyleakin lighthouse of 1857. This is now disused and partly obscured by the bridge. Author Gavin Maxwell bought the island in 1963 to create a zoo for west Highland birds and mammals. He lived in the keeper's cottage. Teko, the last otter from *Ring of Bright Water*, is buried here.

A less spectacular bridge brings the

↑ Caisteal Maol at Kyleakin.

← The Kyle of Lochalsh inshore lifeboat launches from the old ferry slipway to attend a rescue call.

A87 to the island from the Plock of Kyle with its golf course. For smaller craft there is a route between Eilean a' Mhal and various smaller islets and reefs round towards Loch Carron and the northern side of Inner Sound.

↓ The Skye Bridge, now toll free.

DISTANCE
24km from Faddoch to Eilean a' Mhal

OS 1:50,000 SHEET
25 Glen Carron & Glen Affric
33 Loch Alsh, Glen Shiel & Loch Hourn

TIDAL CONSTANTS
Dornie Bridge: HW Dover −0440,
LW Dover −0420
Kyle of Lochalsh: HW Dover −0440,
LW Dover −0430

SEA AREA
Hebrides

RESCUE
Inshore lifeboat: Kyle of Lochalsh
All weather lifeboats: Mallaig, Portree

29 LOCH HARPORT

LEAVING THE BEST BEHIND

LOCH HARPORT

It is the dramatic backdrop of Skye's Cuillin Hills that provides the outstanding scenery here, the rounded Red Cuillin starkly different from the jagged peaks of the Black Cuillin. The River Drynoch loses its momentum after the B8009 bridge at Satran and opens out to become Loch Harport. Launching is possible at either Satran or Drynoch when the tide is in, but the first 1.4km drains. Carbost is a better option.

Bràigh Coille na Droighniche provides a steep north side to the loch, but the south side is rather more gentle, with the Vikisgill Burn joining at Satran and a hillside cemetery at Merkadale standing on the lochside below Dùn Merkadale and a war memorial. Birdlife includes golden and white-tailed sea eagles.

Yachtsmen and coach parties are attracted to the Talisker distillery with its malt-drying kilns facing onto the loch. The distillery was moved here in 1830 and produces a single malt, although most is blended and exported.

A track leads along the shoreline at Carbostbeag past a floating pontoon walkway to a slipway and a high jetty

↑ The head of the loch at low water.

↓ Looking down the loch from Merkadale.

with a picnic table on top, facing across the loch to 196m Uchd Mòr.

The Minginish peninsula on the south side drops down from 416m Stockval and 369m Arnaval. These are hidden by the steep woods that rise from the rocky shoreline past Fernilea. There are volcanic pipes, and a rock takes the form of a bear's head a little further along. Being smaller hills, Cnoc Dubh Heilla and Cnoc Glas Heilla are not seen, even though they are close to the water at Portnalong.

↑ The Black Cuillin beyond Satran.

← One of the lava pipes.

↓ The Talisker distillery at Carbost.

north side before Rubha na h-Uamha take some protection from Bracadale Point. The Victorian Gesto Farm has a circular henhouse heated by a chimney up the centre. Past occupation of the area is shown by a broch, a chambered cairn and Dùn Beag, one of the best preserved brochs on Skye. The current small communities of Coillore, Bracadale, Balgown, Struan and Struanmore merge into each other to form what is still no more than a village.

Flows out through the narrows start

↑ The jetty at Portnalong.

→ The small light is easy to spot on Ardtreck Point.

↓ Fish cages in the bay at Portnalong.

Glas Bheinn drops from its 231m summit to Beinn Dubh with Dùn Taimh and finally to the isolated Cnoc Mhàirtein which falls steeply to the north side of the loch.

Fish farms are situated off Rubha Bàn and the pier at the end of an arm of the B8009 gives some protection to Port nan Long. A light on a white metal tower on Ardtreck Point is low but very conspicuous for inbound boats.

Gesto Bay and Loch Beag on the

4h 40min before Dover high water and flows in start 1h 20min after Dover high water at up to 1km/h (1 knot). North of Port Beag a windfarm is seen, but the view is more restful to the north-west, dominated by Healabhals Mhòr and Bheag. Macleod's Tables North and South respectively are both of flat-topped basalt lavas, the former at 489m, apparently truncated by a giant to provide a table and bed for St Columba.

Oronsay, which also has flattened strata, lies off Ullinish Point, to which it is connected by a causeway once the tide drops. At the east end it has a reef on which there are breakers in all but the finest weather. The Castle pillar is also prominent.

↑ Oronsay in Loch Bracadale.

DISTANCE
11km from Satran to Oronsay

OS 1:50,000 SHEETS
(23 North Skye)
32 South Skye & Cuillin Hills

TIDAL CONSTANTS
Loch Harport: HW Dover −0410,
LW Dover −0450

SEA AREA
Hebrides

RESCUE
Inshore lifeboat: Kyle of Lochalsh
All weather lifeboat: Barra Island

30 LOCH SNIZORT BEAG

INFLUENTIAL PEOPLE

Just before entering Loch Snizort Beag, the little Loch Snizort, the River Snizort passes a ruined chapel, Snizort Cathedral or the Church of St Columba, named after the saint who preached from a nearby rock known as St Columba's rock.

The river drops over a man-made weir at Skeabost and can have strong flows. Otherwise, flows in the loch are very weak. The head of the loch drains for 2km to leave a sea of wrack. Ebb flows begin 4h 40min before Dover high water and the flood begins 1h 40min after Dover high water.

↓ The River Snizort drops into Loch Snizort Beag at Skeabost.

To the east of the loch the land rises to 552m Ben Dearg at the southern end of the Trotternish spine. Clach Ard has one of the best Pictish standing stones on Skye, with rod, mirror and comb symbols. The Cuillin lie to the south but are hidden initially by the foreground. Rhododendrons add colour with a more subtle shade of pink from the thrift along the shoreline.

Skeabost was where poet Mary MacPherson grew up. A large woman physically, she became the most prolific Gaelic poet of the 19th century and a strong supporter of land reform.

Skeabost House, now a hotel, stands on the bank like a white castle. Another prominent white building by the water

is the Free Church. Angus Smith, the minister in 1965, led the opposition to the introduction of a Sunday ferry service for Skye.

Grazing land slopes down on each side of the loch, bracken, gorse and foxgloves breaking up the grass. A cairn below Tote House faces across to Bernisdale, to where the Australian boat designer Iain Oughtred moved to design small wooden boats.

Park Bernisdale is an old crofting settlement, and not enhanced by the machinery that has been pushed down into the loch and left to rust.

The Dùn Cruinn fort had a commanding view over the lower loch to Skerinish Quay, now disused, and Loch Eyre, one of three arms branching off the loch. A standing stone, a cairn, Eyre and 348m Beinn a Chapuill also overlook Loch Eyre from various distances. Beyond another cairn, a lane at Romesdal allows public access via a gate

to the shoreline, a facility rather lacking elsewhere on this loch.

The Aird places an arm round Loch Treaslane on the west side of Loch Snizort Beag, rocks off Aird Point being used by seals.

Kingsburgh House was occupied by the factor of Sir Alexander Macdonald and provided a night's shelter for Prince Charlie on his way to Raasay.

↑ Ben Dearg rises above Loch Eyre while Loch Snizort Beag passes to the right of Dùn Cruinn.

↓ The Free Church at Skeabost.

→ The west side of the mouth of the loch, which leads down to Lyndale Point.

While the east shore continues to have sloping grazing, with a small wind turbine and a boathouse below the Dùn Adhamh fort site at Kingsburgh, the west shore becomes increasingly more rocky, bold and steep to Lyndale Point. The only exception is where another small sea loch runs in between Rubha nan Cudaigean and Seal Rock to Knott.

The River Hinnisdal discharges into Am Bagh-dhùin, around which are Prince Charles' Well and the sites of hut circles, a broch, Caisteal Ùisdein and various other forts. Eilean Beag is the last outcrop as Loch Snizort Beag joins Loch Snizort itself with the Ascrib Islands ahead.

↓ Eilean Beag as Loch Snizort Beag enters Loch Snizort.

DISTANCE_____
10km from Skeabost to Eilean Beag

OS 1:50,000 SHEET_____
23 North Skye

TIDAL CONSTANTS_____
Loch Snizort (Uig Bay):
HW Dover −0440, LW Dover −0420

SEA AREA_____
Hebrides

RESCUE_____
Inshore lifeboat:
Kyle of Lochalsh
All weather lifeboat: Portree

LOCH SLIGACHAN

ONE OF THE BEST WATER CROSSROADS IN SCOTLAND

LOCH SLIGACHAN

The Sligachan Hotel has been a climbing centre since Victorian times. It not only holds a conspicuous position in the fork between the A87 and A863, one of the most important road junctions on Skye, but footpaths radiate out to the Black Cuillin for climbers and through Glen Sligachan for those wanting to walk at low level. The River Sligachan rises on Sgùrr nan Gillean and flows north through the glen, providing the easiest route into the heart of the Black Cuillin.

No hotel is better placed to serve mountaineers, which is why the mountain rescue centre is located behind the hotel.

Its facilities include the large Seumas' Bar, a selection of 400 whiskies (sometimes causing staff some problems in locating a chosen tipple) and a playground for youngsters left behind while parents have their minds on higher things. The Cuillin Brewery is also sited at the hotel.

A campsite at the head of Loch Sligachan is well used by climbers. From here the water turns more to the east, becoming tidal some 700m below the A87 crossing. In fact, the head of the loch drains for some 1.3km and the rocks in the shallow channels can be enough to render them unnavigable. Sheep can

↓ The Black Cuillin towering over the head of Loch Sligachan.

flooding from 1h 40min after Dover high water. Of more concern are the heavy squalls that can result from cold air descending from the high peaks or the prevailing wind blowing through from Loch Brittle.

The A87 follows the south side of the loch past the foot of 775m Glamaig and there are several places where portable craft can be launched from beside the road and vehicles left. The north side has

↑ An Leitir with the Eas Ruadh fall that flows from the summit.

→ The Sligachan Hotel, Skye's climbing centre.

→ Glamaig on the south side of Loch Sligachan.

be isolated on islands at high water, although they seem fairly relaxed about the problem.

Flows are imperceptible as far as the entrance to the loch, ebbing from 4h 40min before Dover high water and

no more than a footpath following the green wall of An Leitir, which flattens out at the top to the 444m summit of Ben Lee. A disused quarry on the south side faces where the Eas Ruadh flows down from the summit of Ben Lee, and a waterfall has stripped the mountainside back to bare rock.

Sconser is the vehicle ferry terminal for Raasay. Rebuilt in 2013, it has toilets and free parking, even for non-ferry users, and a steep second slipway, which leads down to the rocky beach. For portable craft, a less accessible alternative is at the end of the B883 at Peinchorran before Rubh' an Tòrra Mhòir on the north side of the loch.

There is a golf course on the south side behind Rubha Garbh, followed at the mouth of the Abhainn Torra-mhicaig by the former Sconser Quarry, which spreads across the road. It might be tempting to blame this for the state of the road, but it does not improve as it winds its way round Rubh' an Uillt Dharaich to Moll and back up Loch Ainort.

Ahead is one of the best water crossroads in Scotland. The view back along Loch Sligachan is to the Cuillin and ahead through Caol Mòr is to the Inner Sound, the Crowlin Islands and the Applecross peaks. To the south-east, Loch na Cairidh and Caolas Scalpay run between Scalpay and 732m Beinn na Caillich while north-west the Narrows of Raasay lead inside Raasay to

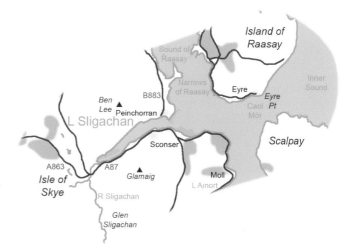

the Sound of Raasay and the Trotternish peninsula with its dramatic rock formations.

The ferry pier on Raasay used to be an iron ore terminal from 1913 to 1919 when it was served by a narrow gauge railway.

↓ The former Sconser Quarry below Meall Buidhe.

↑ Eyre Point lighthouse, looking back towards the Cuillin peaks.

Distinctive near Rubha na Cloiche is the art studio of Barbara Martin, sandwiched between a pair of stone walls with a clear front and pierced by unusually shaped door and window openings.

Terns fish off Eyre. Eyre Point is marked by a lighthouse, a small square tower, as the Caol Mòr channel opens into the Inner Sound.

Facing, on the south side, is Scalpay, with Camas na Geadaig indented between Rubh' a' Chonnaidh and Rubh' a' Chinn Mhòir. The heather-covered island is used for deer and sheep grazing and seals are present in its water. Submarines might also be seen in the Inner Sound, this being an exercise area.

The views are excellent in all directions, surely none better than that faced by Barbara Martin's studio on the island of Raasay.

↓ Artist Barbara Martin's studio on Raasay.

DISTANCE_____
10km from Sligachan Hotel to Eyre Pt

OS 1:50,000 SHEETS_____
(24 Raasay & Applecross)
32 South Skye & Cuillin Hills

TIDAL CONSTANTS_____
Portree: Dover −0440

SEA AREA_____
Hebrides

RESCUE_____
Inshore lifeboat: Kyle of Lochalsh
All weather lifeboat: Portree

LOCH CARRON

MONSTERS AND A SPECTACULAR RAILWAY FINALE

As his contribution to *Great Railway Journeys of the World*, trainspotter Sir Michael Palin offers Euston to Kyle of Lochalsh, the 'spectacular grand finale' being the run down the side of Loch Carron. The view from the water is even better than from the train as both sides of the loch are seen.

Reducing the railway line to single track in the 1960s freed up enough space to insert the single lane A890 down the south-east side of the loch. Until then traffic had used Telford's road, the A896 on the other side of the loch, and the ferry further down, a terrible bottleneck with no Sunday service, only avoided by

LOCH CARRON

← Water spurts up from underground at high water.

↓ Looking up to the head of Loch Carron.

taking a 220km detour. The ferry had to be brought back into use in 2011 after rockfalls closed the A890.

Beyond the golf course, Lochcarron or Jeantown was begun in 1800 in imitation

↑ Slumbay Harbour serves as an anchorage.

↓ The disused ferry slipway at Stromemore.

↓ Lochcarron, no longer on the road to Kyle of Lochalsh.

of government fishing villages such as Ullapool, but even though there are cod, ling, mackerel, pollock and skate in the loch it was ultimately unsuccessful. It was badly damaged by the closure of Strome Ferry, which diverted much traffic away from the village but benefited for several years from oil platform construction. Near the Lochcarron Hotel is a slipway into the loch with an anchorage in Slumbay Harbour.

Facing Sgeir Fhada is a cave and then Attadale Gardens with waterfalls, ponds, a Japanese garden, rare trees and shrubs and a geodesic dome housing exotic ferns near the River Attadale confluence. Càrn nan Iomairean rises to 486m, before which there is a short avalanche protection roof over the railway and A890, one of only two in Britain.

There are hut circles below the Black Mare's Rock on the north-west side of the

loch. When active, Lochcarron Weavers, the other side of the wood, claimed to be the world's largest manufacturer of authentic tartans, although the weaving is now undertaken in Selkirk.

Submarine cables cross the loch and seals and herons are present. Fish cages are located near Ardnarff.

Bad a' Chreamha rises 395m above the Strome Narrows, outgoing from 4h 20min before Dover high water and ingoing from 1h 40min after Dover high water to 6km/h (3 knots). Rusting in the shallows is a diminutive ferry, its rotating car deck lying out at an angle as if resting on one elbow. The car ferry slip remains on the far side of the Strome Castle ruins at Stromemore.

Stromeferry, marked by the pointed 286m peak of Am Meallan above, was the railway terminus for the first 40 years, connecting with ferries to the Hebrides, until the line was extended to Kyle of Lochalsh.

Creag Mhaol drops steeply to the fishing village of Portchullin, a raised beach 25–30m high running round to the Allt Cadh an Eas.

The 2m white triangular Leacanashie Beacon, on a concrete base, is on the north side of the narrows. From here the loch widens again and becomes dotted with reefs and islets, starting

↑ Portchullin with Carn a' Bhealaich Mhòir beyond.

with the Strome Islands and Eilean an t-Sratha. These have wooded terraces up to 26m high, as have Ardaneaskan with a steep, raised beach at the same level. Ardaneaskan also has a museum.

Heather, primroses and rhododendrons are found along the south shore, where the 350m basalt cliffs of Creag an Duilisg extend to the 343m Carn a' Bhealaich Mhòir with its mast. The stone beacon on Ulluva is hard to see. Birch Rock is in the fairway and there is a 2m white triangular Duncraig beacon. Duncraig Island has pink and purple coral sand, which used to be used as fertilizer. Approach on land to Duncraig station is through the grounds of the stone Duncraig Castle in the woods, which is now used as a college.

Eilean na Beinne, off Rubha Alasdair Ruaidh, helps shelter the southern side of Loch Reraig, which has the Loch Reraig beacon on it.

Bogha Dubh Sgeir and Sgeir Golach each have 3m red pile beacons and there

DISTANCE_____
16km from Tullich to Sgeir Bhuidhe

OS 1:50,000 SHEETS_____
24 Raasay & Applecross
25 Glen Carron & Glen Affric

TIDAL CONSTANTS_____
Plockton: HW Dover −0430,
LW Dover −0420

SEA AREA_____
Hebrides

RESCUE_____
Inshore lifeboat: Kyle of Lochalsh
All weather lifeboat: Portree

is an old white lighthouse on Eilean a' Chait, the first of the Cat Islands. Plockton, which faces east, was a schooner trading port and has palm trees, an indication of its sheltered position.

The last of the skerries in the centre of the loch are the Sgeir Bhuidhe pair, almost under the flight path for Plockton Airfield, before Loch Carron is joined by Loch Kishorn.

→ A seal resting on Sgeir Bhuidhe.

UPPER LOCH TORRIDON

DARK ARTS AND THE OLDEST ROCKS

33

The kingdom of the westward waters,
* wherein when we swam we knew*
The waves that we clove were boundless,
* the wind on our brows that blew*
Had swept no land and no lake, and had
* warred not on tower or on tree,*
But came on us hard out of heaven,
* and alive with the soul of the sea.*
ALGERNON CHARLES SWINBURNE

Tides rise up the River Torridon as far as the A896 bridge but below high water the water is usually shallow and littered with a graveyard of rocks. The Allt a' Choire Dhuibh Mhòir rises in Torridon Forest and becomes the River Torridon as it flows in a circle and then heads west across the Highlands. The top 700m drains and flows are generally very weak, although the loch is subject to squalls with any wind.

All around are the 75,000,000-year-old peaks of old red Torridonian sandstone, capped with white quartzite summits.

There are red and roe deer. On the edge of Torridon is the Deer Museum, including antlers and poachers' snares. There is a Torridon Countryside Centre, too.

The head of the loch sees herons, curlews, oystercatchers, herring gulls and cormorants, with Norway lobster burrows and razor

UPPER LOCH
TORRIDON

← Beinn Damh next to the head of the loch.

↓ Annat at the foot of Beinn na h-Eaglaise.

→ Tom na Gruagaich and Beinn Dearg on the north side of Loch Torridon.

↓ Rubha na h-Àirde Glaise at the northern side of the narrows.

shells on the beach and barnacles, limpets and mussels on the rocks.

Torridon House, at the mouth of the Abhainn Coire Mhic Nòbuil, was threatened by a fire in 2011 but survived. Also here is a church with a square belfry.

The southern side of the loch is extensively indented and carved by rivers. The Allt Coire Roill flows down from Ben-damph Forest, Òb Gorm Mòr and Òb Gorm Beag are below 687m Sgùrr Bana Mhoraire and the River Balgy drains Loch Damh. Camas a' Chlàrsair and Òb Mheallaidh, off which a fish farm is situated, eat into the foot of the 534m Ben Shieldaig ridge. Camas an Lèim cuts into the east side of the peninsula reaching to Eilean a' Chaoil, which has a drying reef at the southern end and constrains the southern side of the narrows.

Below 986m Beinn Alligin the Abhainn Alligin flows into the loch at Inveralligin. Rubh' a' Ghiubhais divides

Òb a' Bhràighe from Port an Lagaidh below the village of Alligin Shuas.

Forming the northern side of the narrows is Rubha na h-Àirde Glaise with a ruin at its tip. Flows begin outwards 4h 30min before Dover high water and inwards 2h after Dover high water and can reach 4km/h (2 knots).

Loch Shieldaig joins beyond the narrows. The white houses of Shieldaig are conspicuous towards the head of the loch.

Sròn a' Mahàis and Màs Diabaig provide another narrowing before joining Loch Torridon itself, Loch Diabaig and Loch Beag providing symmetry as they cut into the head of Loch Torridon each side of these narrows. Heather covers the hillsides and seals watch from below.

↑ Camas Ruadh forms the southern side of the narrows, but a cut through to the south of Eilean a' Chaoil leads to Loch Shieldaig.

↓ Shieldaig lies at the head of Loch Shieldaig.

DISTANCE
12km from Torridon to Sròn a' Mahàis

OS 1:50,000 SHEETS
24 Raasay & Applecross
25 Glen Carron & Glen Affric

TIDAL CONSTANTS
Shieldaig: HW Dover −0430,
LW Dover −0420

SEA AREA
Hebrides

RESCUE
Inshore lifeboat: Kyle of Lochalsh
All weather lifeboat: Portree

34

LOCH MAREE

PERHAPS SCOTLAND'S FINEST INLAND LOCH

LOCH MAREE

→ Tangled roots beside the road.

Show me Airigh 'n Eilean,
*   below me Loch Maree*
Oh leave me to my solitude
*   and let me wander free*
To climb the rocky
*   mountains and to search*
*   the glen below*
For a fine ten pointer or
*   a royal 'O'*

Take me where I faintly see
*   the distant Isle of Lewis*
In all this world, there's
*   only one place I would*
*   choose*
To represent the beauty of my
*   lovely homeland fair*
The Loch Maree islands from the
*   heights of Ardlair*
KENNETH C MACKENZIE

↓ Beinn a' Mhuinidh overlooks Gleann Bianasdail.

Flowing north-west in a straight line, this is the last remaining large loch in the north Highlands not to be used for hydroelectric power. Glaciation has resulted in some dramatic scenery.

The loch became more fashionable after a visit in 1877 by Queen Victoria. Accordionist Fergie MacDonald took Kenneth C Mackenzie's *Loch Maree Islands* to the Scottish No 1 in 1966, giving further publicity. Research by Sheffield University suggested it was the least sunny place in Britain in 2011. However, author Alfred Wainwright thought it the loveliest of Scotland's freshwater lochs.

The loch needs to be seen from the water or from the long and committing footpath on the north-east side. Although the A832 follows much of the south-west shore it is extensively hidden by trees. Yet the road is close enough to be banked up by stone walls at the edge of the loch in places. Be aware that parking areas off the road are limited.

The one nearest to the head of the loch is marked for the Beinn Eighe National Nature Reserve, established in 1951 as Britain's first. A nature trail and a mountain trail lead through woods and, particularly, through the pines, this being one of the most westerly remaining sections of the old Caledonian pine

sheilch, perhaps a large eel.

The mountains to the south are some of Europe's oldest and some of Scotland's finest. As a result of earth movements

forest, pines at Coille na Glas-Leitire being up to 360 years of age. Pines along the shore can have gnarled roots above the ground. Wildlife inhabiting the area includes red deer, pine martens, wildcats, golden eagles, buzzards, ravens, crossbills, great crested grebes, blue Aeshna hawkers and golden-ringed dragonflies, northern eggar moths and midges. Oaks on the north-east side of the loch are the most northerly on the west side of the country.

There are Willoughby's char in the loch. In 1952 it produced the heaviest recorded sea trout catch, 8.8kg. It is also supposed to have a monster, Muc-

Beinn Eighe's Torridonian sandstone is on top of quartzite rocks, which are younger. The steep and rugged Meall a' Ghiubhais, on the flank of Beinn Eighe, is itself 887m high.

The Abhainn an Fhasaigh is one of two water channels down from Lochan Fada,

↑ Slioch with its magnificent outline.

dividing the peaks of Kinlochewe Forest, including 692m Beinn a' Mhuinidh, from 980m Slioch, the spear. Cloud descending between Slioch's pinnacles can resemble cream being poured over it in slow motion. Below, the loch can be as little as 700m wide but more than 110m deep.

Beyond the River Grudie is a small island with the remains of a castle, even the heap of stones now being barely visible. A private pier is used by a small boat to serve Letterewe House on the north-east side. First, the Abhainn na Fùirneis descends from the peaks of Letterewe Forest to the blast furnace founded by Sir George Hay in 1607, one of the first ironworks in the north, which used charcoal from local timber. During the Second World War pines were felled by the Pioneer Corps from

→ Little remains of the castle on its island.

Newfoundland and British Honduras as part of the war effort. At Letterewe the Allt Folais joins below a waterfall.

The loch has a 3km-wide bay to the south-west, 6km long and studded with islands, starting with Eilean Mhic an Fhùlaraich and Eilean Eachainn. Although relatively small, Isle Maree was probably the most important historically. Saint Maelrubha set up a hermitage on it, later a chapel, and it was used until the 19th century for rites, which included bull sacrifice and worshipping at a sacred well. Lunatics were to be cured by drinking at the holy well and being dipped in the loch three times a day for many days. This treatment was most effective at curing patients on St Maelrubha's Day, 25 August, perhaps because the water temperature ought to have been at its mildest then.

Among the larger islands are Eilean Sùbhainn, Garbh Eilean and Eilean

Ruaridh Mòr, which has a small forest nature reserve in remnant pine wood. Eilean Sùbhainn is unique in Britain in having its own lochan with an island, like Russian dolls. Here are some of the least disturbed native pine woods in Scotland with larch, juniper and heather about. These are breeding sites for black-throated and great northern divers, with restrictions on landing during the breeding season.

A low peninsula reaches into the loch

↑ Isle Maree, an island with a long history.

↓ The peaks of Flowerdale Forest, seen from beyond the islands.

→ Anchored in
Tollie Bay.

below 720m Beinn Airigh Charr, but the dramatic skyline is that of Flowerdale Forest to the south with an expanse of jagged peaks. Well placed to make the most of the view is the modern house at Ardlair with its jetty.

At Rubh' Aird an Anail the loch narrows down again to 700m wide. The foot of the loch has a hump covered with dark trees. Beyond a couple of metal poles marking shallow rocks, the River Ewe leaves on the north-east side past a boathouse.

For portable boats a useful take out is at the back of Tollie Bay where a narrow unmarked lane leads down from the A832 past Tollie Farm and between walls of bracken to very limited parking.

DISTANCE_____
20km from Taagan to Tollie Bay

OS 1:50,000 SHEET_____
19 Gairloch & Ullapool

↓ Looking up the
loch from Tollie Bay.

LOCH EWE

EXOTIC PLANTS AND ARCTIC SHIPPING

LOCH EWE

The River Ewe meets tidal water at Poolewe, the biggest rapids in its 3km length being under the A832 bridge after which it turns a corner between rock walls to open out into Loch Ewe. Unexpectedly, strong flows continue in a north-easterly direction, parallel to the main road.

For portable craft, launching here can be undertaken from a lay-by at Londubh, down a rocky bank and across a beach covered with wrack. Perhaps easier options are Aultbea, behind the Isle of Ewe, or from other jetties dotted around the loch. This guide concentrates on the west side of the wide loch, which is followed by the B8057, although only directly accessible to the water on rare occasions. This Highland sea loch runs north-west with the west shore steep-to.

On the east side of this first inlet is Inverewe Garden, one of the finest gardens in Scotland. It was founded in 1862 by 20-year-old Osgood Mackenzie on a site far from promising, a red sandstone peninsula covered with acidic black peat, some heather and a single stunted dwarf willow. The big advantage of the 20ha garden is the mild climate, the North Atlantic Drift allowing him to

↓ Beinn Airigh Charr and other peaks provide a backdrop for Loch Ewe, seen from Boor Rocks.

↑ The River Ewe emerges into Loch Ewe at Poolewe.

grow exotic plants from many countries, including palm trees, eucalyptus trees more than 24m high, a 15m magnolia, bamboo, rhododendrons and the national collection of *Olearias*. Firstly, Mackenzie had to plant a shelter belt of Scots and Corsican pines and these are what are seen from the water. In 1952 his daughter presented the garden to the National Trust for Scotland.

Boor Rocks, near the west side of the inlet, attract some of the loch's birdlife, which includes cormorants, oystercatchers, razorbills, guillemots and herons. Seals inhabit the waters, which have coalfish, cod, haddock, pollack and lion's mane jellyfish.

The loch is a submarine exercise area and has had a

→ Low cloud drifts past the jetty at Naast.

significant naval history, being a Second World War assembly point for North Atlantic convoys, sending 19 of them to Archangel. It is still refuelling NATO ships on the east side of the loch.

Naast has a jetty with small fishing boats drawn up on the beach and there is another pier at Inverasdale, where the

↑ Coigach peaks seen from the loch.

coast turns north. Bays have pink sand, backed by bracken, and Midtown has a conspicuous wind turbine.

A footpath along the former line of the coast continues in a north-west direction to meet the Minch 2km east of Rubha Reidh. To its south-west the land continues to rise steeply to a relative plateau, but to its north-east, on both sides of the loch, it is much lower with frequent lochans.

The flow reaches its maximum rate off An Sguiteach, where the Isle of Ewe is at its nearest to constrict the flow. A normal maximum is 1km/h (1 knot), but the rate may be affected by discharge from Loch Maree. Flows out are from 4h 20min before Dover high water and in from 2h 10min after Dover high water.

Mellangaun is opposite the Sgeir an Araig, after which the loch opens out.

DISTANCE_____
10km from Poolewe to Mellangaun

OS 1:50,000 SHEET_____
19 Gairloch & Ullapool

TIDAL CONSTANTS_____
Gairloch: HW Dover −0430,
LW Dover −0420

SEA AREA_____
Hebrides

RESCUE_____
Inshore lifeboat: Kyle of Lochalsh
All weather lifeboat: Stornoway

Ahead, Cove, a possible landing place, has a cave that was formerly used as a place of worship. At the end of the road there are the remains of the fortifications. Indeed, there was a wartime submarine boom placed across the entrance to the loch to prevent submarine entry.

36 LITTLE LOCH BROOM

LOW-TECH LIVING

LITTLE LOCH BROOM

The top kilometre of the loch drains, but it is a wet area, experiencing 1.8m of rain per year.

There are Scots pines, but many of the trees planted for a house in 1769 are unusual for the area, such as beech, chestnut and lime. There are red squirrels in the woods, while the loch has cormorants, curlews, razor shells and mussels.

Behind the Dundonnell Hotel, accompanied by a mountain rescue post, the mountains rise to Strathnasheallag Forest with An Teallach, the anvil or forge, at 1,062m with cloud usually

coming off the summit. However, this is hidden by Sgùrr Fiona at 1,069m, which is only 1.2km from the loch. Except at the head of the loch the coasts are steep-to.

After Sròn Creag na Ceapaich the loch widens to Kildonan below a standing stone and, more obviously, to Badrallach below 545m Cnoc a' Bhaid-rallaich and 635m Beinn Ghobhlach.

A section of the flatter shoreline on the south side runs between Camusnagaul and the Allt Airdeasaidh where the Ardessie Falls are close to the loch. Above is the round top of Sàil Mhór, the big heel, at 767m. This is an area

↓ Beinn Ghoblach on the north side of the loch.

where south-westerly winds can bring dangerous squalls and whirlwinds.

Not seen is the Conger Stack in the centre of the loch, rising from 50m depth to have only 7m of water over its top.

Fish farms are sited along the south side of the loch.

JL Henderson's book *Kayak to Cape Wrath* describes bathing in a tin bath at the former Badcaul youth hostel. As late as the 1960s a campsite boasted of its

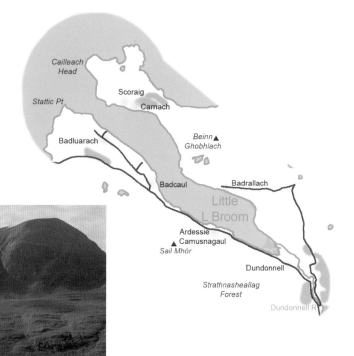

flush toilet. The hut was built over a stream running down to the loch.

The loch sides become lower from here. Badluarach has Victorian houses and modern bungalows above a jetty and sheep on the hillsides.

Carnach and Scoraig were resettled in the 1960s by people looking for an alternative lifestyle, using wind and solar power, growing organic crops and declining the offer of an access road. The indications are of a thriving community.

Flows start out between Leac an Ime and Corran Sgoraig 4h 20min before Dover high water and in 2h 10min after Dover high water at up to 2km/h (1 knot).

← Sáil Mhór dominates the centre of the loch with An Teallach beyond.

↓ Looking down the loch from Dundonnell.

↑ A cave at the mouth of the loch.

↑ Scoraig is an unusual isolated community.

With easterly winds, the strengths may be greater than forecast.

Kelp, urchins, seals and otters are in the clear water, great northern, red- and black-throated and white-billed divers may be on it and the hillsides have horses and wild goats.

The loch discharges into the Minch between Stattic Point and Cailleach Head with its lighthouse.

↓ Looking out from the loch with Priest Island in the distance.

DISTANCE_____
13km from Dundonnell to Corran Sgoraig

OS 1:50,000 SHEET_____
19 Gairloch & Ullapool

TIDAL CONSTANTS_____
Tanera Mòr: HW Dover −0410, LW Dover −0420

SEA AREA_____
Hebrides

RESCUE_____
Inshore lifeboat: Kyle of Lochalsh
All weather lifeboat: Lochinver

LOCH BROOM

AN 18TH-CENTURY NEW TOWN

LOCH BROOM

Ullapool sits in ephemeral neatness
Parties arriving at wool shops and
  cafes
Bargains in tweeds and bar lunches
  for pleasure.
JOAN PITTOCK WESSON

The River Broom becomes tidal just before meeting Loch Broom. Razorbills nest, there is a white-headed subspecies of long-tailed tit, mallards and herons are present in quantity and mammals include red squirrels and pine martens. The top kilometre of the loch drains but air and water gush from around vegetation at high water. There are jellyfish to be found in the clear water of the loch.

This is the longest sea loch in the north-west Highlands and fjord-like in character. The top end has squalls in windy weather, especially from the south-east. Otherwise it is sheltered.

A minor road on the west side serves Letters, Ardindrean, Rhiroy and Blarnalearoch, where it ends. Most traffic is on the east bank, where Ardcharnich rests below 642m Meall Dubh.

Rhiroy has the Iron Age Pictish broch ruin of Dùn an Ruigh Ruadh, although a fish farm in the loch is more conspicuous these days.

Below 558m Beinn Eilideach is the Leckmelm Shrubbery & Arboretum of 1870 with walled garden, rare trees, rhododendrons and azaleas.

↓ Cnoc an Droighinn stands above Ardindrean.

Overlooking An Acarsaid with its wreck and moored boats is the Dùn Lagaidh ruin, an Iron Age vitrified fort. Seals will not be far away.

Flows can reach 2km/h (1 knot) through the narrowest part of the loch, out from 4h 20min before Dover high water and in from 2h 10min after Dover high water. Otherwise they

↓ A CalMac ferry from Stornoway arrives at Ullapool.

↙ Looking down the loch towards Beinn Eilideach.

are weak through the loch.

Beinn nam Ban reaches 580m opposite the Braes of Ullapool.

Ullapool was founded in 1788 by the British Society of Extending the Fisheries as a herring centre with Tobermory and Oban after the success of Rodel on Harris. Up to the 18th century the herring had circulated round the loch, a fact discovered and exploited by the Dutch. Herring fishing declined from 1820 and had finished by 1880, although there are salmon, trout, whiting and skate in the loch. The town has 1.6m of rain per year but little snow or frost.

The only major town in north-west Scotland, Ullapool's plans were approved by Telford. The Ullapool Museum is in a

DISTANCE_____
15km from Inverlael to Rubha Cadail

OS 1:50,000 SHEETS_____
19 Gairloch & Ullapool
20 Beinn Dearg

TIDAL CONSTANTS_____
Ullapool: Dover −0410

SEA AREA_____
Hebrides

RESCUE_____
Inshore lifeboat: Kessock
All weather lifeboat: Lochinver

← Beinn Ghobhlach on the south side of Loch Broom.

Telford-designed church. The town has a mountain rescue kit. Highland Stoneware is based here, too.

The pier serves a vehicle ferry to Stornoway and a passenger ferry across to Allt na h-Airbhe. There is a white ice plant building on the pier, which is used by the fishing fleet.

Ullapool Point has a light on a 6m grey mast, adjacent to Broomfield Park for caravans. The Ullapool River enters the loch on the north side of the town.

The wreck of a fishing boat lies on the shoreline at Morefield where houses dot the hillside, as they do at Rhue, between the Ben Mór Coigach and the lighthouse at Rubha Cadail. Deer and sheep wander at will. On the south-west side, the loch enters the Minch at Rubha Camas a' Mhaóraich, behind which the land rises away to 635m Beinn Ghobhlach.

→ The lighthouse at Rubha Cadail with Ben Mór Coigach beyond.

LOCH ASSYNT

Or has it come to this,
that this dying landscape belongs
to the dead, the crofters and fighters
and fishermen whose larochs
sink into the bracken
by Loch Assynt and Loch Crocach? –
to men trampled under the hoofs of sheep
and driven by deer to
the ends of the earth – to men whose loyalty
was so great it accepted their own betrayal
by their own chiefs and whose descendants now
are kept in their place
by English businessman and the indifference
of a remote and ignorant government.

NORMAN MACCAIG

Map labels: Quinag · A894 · Glas Bheinn · R Inver · L Assynt · Skiag Br · A837 · Beinn Garbh · Inchnadamph · Inchnadamph Forest

↓ Glas Bheinn runs down to Inchnadamph Forest.

The River Loanan and the River Traligill deliver their peaty waters together to the head of Loch Assynt at Inchnadamph, although they are often too shallow and rocky for boats. The loch runs mostly north-west.

The head of the loch has flowers in summer, which are almost alpine in appearance. The extensive limestone results in the presence here of many rare plants.

A small, pointed monument on the east side near the head of the loch was erected in the 1930s to celebrate the

unravelling of the geology of the north-west Highlands by Ben Peach and John Horne. There are plenty of dramatic examples of geological formations in sight. These include the peaks of Inchnadamph Forest and a cliff running behind Inchnadamph, where the Assynt Mountain Rescue post is based.

The A837 follows the north side of the loch, attracting noisy motorbikes, although many of them head up the A894 from Skiag Bridge, leaving the rest of the loch quieter. Before the junction the rockface is sheeted with wire mesh to contain rockfalls.

A convenient place to launch is near Calda House, where there is parking above the beach. Calda House is now just a large skeleton. Known as the White House, it was built in 1726 for the laird, Kenneth MacKenzie II, whose wife found Ardvreck Castle too austere. Her extravagances and the cost of supporting the Royalist cause resulted in the house having to be sold a decade later to clear debts. It was bought by the Earl of Sutherland, but MacKenzie supporters swore that no Sutherland should live there and attacked and destroyed it. As the first modern house of its kind in the area, it acted as a model for other large houses that were built subsequently.

Ardvreck Castle was begun about 1590

↑ Ben More Assynt and the cliffs behind Inchnadamph.

↓ Ardvreck Castle remains with Quinag behind.

↑ Quinag's western wall of rock.

↗ Cnoc a' Ghlinnein to the south of the loch.

by Angus Mor III. Its final destruction resulted from a lightning strike in 1795.

Other ruins include a kiln barn for drying grain, a grain mill with a horizontal millstone driven by water and a chambered cairn more than 4,000 years old, which was excavated in 1925.

The loch reaches its greatest depth of more than 80m to the west of the castle. Beinn Gharbh, at 539m, is the most conspicuous peak on the south side of the loch, but the north side has 776m

Glas Bheinn, while Quinag peaks at 808m with various arms and a western wall that runs north for 5km.

Views are extensive because there is limited tree cover near the loch, although there are outcrops of pines along some sections of shoreline. Eilean Assynt is in the centre of a larger inlet, but there are many secluded bays, especially on the south side of the loch.

At Rubh' an Alt-toir the loch turns sharply to the south-west. The final take out to the A837 is 400m short of the sluices, where a large boat has been drawn up at the back of an inlet with roadside parking above.

The River Inver leaves through wooden sluices. It may be possible to shoot the wooden sluices, where the drop is about 1m, but the river soon afterwards is shallow and rocky in summer conditions.

↑ An island of pines on the south-western arm of Loch Assynt.

DISTANCE
10km from Inchnadamph to Loch na Garbh Uidhe

OS 1:50,000 SHEET
15 Loch Assynt

← The sluices at the end of the loch.

39 LOCH A' CHÀIRN BHÀIN

MINI SUBMARINES AND BRITAIN'S HIGHEST WATERFALL

LOCH A' CHÀIRN BHÀIN

→ The old ferry slipway at Kylesku.

↓ The graceful Kylesku Bridge crosses the loch.

O my first love! You are in my
life forever
Like the Eas-Coul-aulin in
Sutherlandshire
Where the Amhainnan Loch
Bhig burn
Plunges over the desolate slopes
of Leotir Dubh.
HUGH MACDIARMID

The Abhainn an Loch Bhig flows northwest across the Highlands from its source on Beinn Uidhe. As it passes the prominent 494m Stack of Glencoul it is joined by the flow of Eas a' Chùal Aluinn, Britain's highest waterfall at 197m. This important attraction is best approached by boat to Loch Beag and then a 1km walk over rough vegetation up the valley to the foot of the falls.

As Loch Beag enters Loch Glencoul the hills drop away to the west, giving a clear view through to Quinag, of which the distinctive peaks of 808m Sàil Gharbh and 776m Sàil Gorm dominate the view.

Loch Glendhu joins, and near its mouth there are waterfalls as the Maldie Burn descends from Loch an Leathiad Bhuain.

Kylesku used to be an important ferry point, but since 1984 the A894 has been carried across the graceful Kylesku Bridge. This is a prestressed concrete

box structure with a 129m main span carried on V-shaped piers, curving on to Garbh Eilean, from where it is carried north by a conspicuous causeway.

Beyond Uamh Ruaidhridh is Camas na Cusgaig, the fishery jetty. The former jetty on the south side leads up to the Kylesku Hotel, which specialises in local seafood, and to public toilets. Wagtails hop about between the lobster pots. The road serving Eilean na Rainich in North Ferry Bay is now private.

Caolas Cumhann, under the bridge, has flows out from 3h 40min before Dover high water and in from 2h 20min after Dover high water at up to 5km/h (3 knots). The water boils and swirls and there can be dangerous eddies at the sides. There are limpets and barnacles on the rocks, possibly urchins, and kelp can be seen through the clear water.

Loch a' Chàirn Bhàin curves away from Kylestrome with a cairn and a dun near the water.

Bàgh an Duine, between Rubh' an Fhir Lèith and Rubha Ghallascaig, faces out to Eilean a' Ghamhna, notably green

with its covering of grass and bushes.

The loch was used during the Second World War to develop X-Craft, mini submarines with the primary and successful objective of placing explosives on the hull of the *Tirpitz*, Germany's largest ever battleship, as it was moored in a heavily defended Norwegian fjord.

These days jellyfish are found below the surface. Black-backed and herring gulls and cormorants wait on the rocks and deer may be seen among the heather.

By Kerracher Bay are Kerracher Gardens, only accessible by boat.

At its mouth the loch is turned west into Eddrachillis Bay by Duartmore Point, almost an island sheltering Loch Shark below the conifers of Duartmore Forest, and by the islands of Calbha Mòr and Calbha Beag. On the south side of the entrance Eilean Ruairidh, studded with deer tracks, extends the shore of Loch na Mola.

Further off are Oldany Island to the west and a spattering of islands towards Handa Island in the north.

DISTANCE
14km from Loch Beag to Eilean Rairidh

OS 1:50,000 SHEET
15 Loch Assynt

TIDAL CONSTANTS
Lochinver: Dover −0420

SEA AREA
Hebrides

RESCUE
Inshore lifeboat: Kessock
All weather lifeboat: Lochinver

LOCH ERIBOLL

Or farther, where, beneath the northern skies,
Chides wild Loch-Eribol his caverns hoar–
But, be the minstrel judge, they yield the prize
Of desert dignity to that dread shore
SIR WALTER SCOTT

It was Loch 'Orrible to seamen mustering here for convoys during the Second World War, but the best conditions most would see for a long while, if ever. Its remoteness and some of the deepest waters on the western side of Scotland, as much as 64m, with the approach more than 30m deep, made it suitable as a naval base. It was where the German U-boats surrendered to the Royal Navy at the end of the war. Now it is where great northern divers convene for spring passage to Iceland. The name is from the Norse for home on a gravelly beach.

At its head it is fed by a burn that is tidal from the A838 at Polla, where it drops through a narrow slot into Loch Eriboll. The first 800m drains of its clear peaty water to leave sand and shingle. The loch can suffer from violent gusts with south-westerly gales at any season.

To its west are 800m Cranstackie and 772m Beinn Spionnaidh. Other peaks

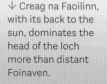

↓ Creag na Faoilinn, with its back to the sun, dominates the head of the loch more than distant Foinaven.

back from the head of the loch include Foinaven with Ganu Mór at 908m. It is Creag na Faoilinn that dominates, however. It is only 286m high but nearly vertical and dark because it faces north just beyond the head of the loch.

Below Creag na Faoilinn is Lochan Havurn cut into flat ground at the head of the loch. There is heather and some fine birch woods with forestry plantation along the west shore at first.

Flows to 1km/h (1 knot) begin out of the loch 3h 20min before Dover high water and in 3h after Dover high water.

Upper Roadstead is sheltered by grassy Rubh' Armli. Beyond, on the east side of the loch, a sand spit runs out from Rubh' Ard Bhaideanach, above which is a hut circle site. Pink cliffs extend along the shore. Marine farms are sited at intervals.

The major feature in the centre of the loch is Eilean Choraidh, grass covered and with a shingle beach at the southern end. It was used for bomber target practice during the Second World War and was fitted with dummy anti-aircraft batteries and smoke generators prior to the sinking of the German battleship *Tirpitz* – Loch Eriboll is similar in shape to Norway's Kaafjord, where the battleship was sheltering.

Laid has crofts on the poor-quality west side of the loch, occupants having been moved from the more fertile east side during the Clearances. This is one of the least inhabited areas of the north coast with much land now idle and sheep outnumbering humans by twenty to one around the loch. Below the crofts there is an occasional modern house standing on the shoreline.

↑ The burn drops into Loch Eriboll at Polla.

← The souterrain entrance above Port Chamuill.

Behind An t-Sròn is the Torr Liath ruined broch. Camus an Dùin runs to Ard Neackie, an island connected to the shore by a finger of land that stops swells coming south. There is a pier, old quarries, limekilns and the landform Geodh' an Sgadain.

↑ The fish farm at
Rubha Ruadh.

souterrain, probably an Iron Age food store, its entrance narrow, low and wet.

The A838 turns east away from the loch, passing Tòrr na Bithe, hut circles and a broch. Below 177m Ben Heilam with its apparently flat summit is White Head with a 5m white tower sector lighthouse, made more conspicuous by a splash of white down the cliff below it.

A' Chléit on the west side is grass covered, an island at high water. Bàgh Loch Sian is occupied by a fish farm. From Rubha Ruadh there are low cliffs, covered with pale green lichen towards Grave Point and giving the appearance of being covered with weathered copper sheeting.

There is also a disused quarry on the west side above Portnancon, where the stone pier is now privately owned and it has been made difficult to turn a vehicle round. Port Chamuill is much more easily accessible with some commercial premises, small craft anchored and an excavated approach at the start of a drying inlet, which does not quite make Eilean Dubh an island. Kelp, wrack, welks and urchins are to be found.

A little way up the side of 422m Meall Meadhonach in the bracken is a

The loch widens out to become a bay, the River Hope entering on the east side beyond Rubh' a' Mhuilt and Sgeir a' Bhuic. Whiten Head can't quite be seen beyond Cnoc Àrd an t-Siùil, but Eilean Clùimhrig stands off the beautiful little harbour of Rispond at the foot of 383m Beinn Ceannabeinne.

↓ Whiten Head seen
from Grave Point.

DISTANCE_____
  11km from Polla to Grave Point

OS 1:50,000 SHEETS_____
  9 Cape Wrath

TIDAL CONSTANTS_____
  Portnancon: Dover −0310

SEA AREA_____
  Fair Isle

RESCUE _____
  Inshore lifeboat: Dornoch
  All weather lifeboat: Thurso

LOCH HOPE

HIGH POINTS FOR MANY

The minor road along the east side of Loch Hope is frequently very busy with the vehicles of mountain climbers. Beside the head of the loch is the pyramid of Ben Hope, at 927m the most northerly of Scotland's 282 Munros and therefore on the tick list of every serious mountain walker and climber.

There are only two places to get off this narrow road to reach the water, each with a sandy beach where anglers moor their boats: one about 800m from the head of the loch and the other some 3km from the start. The first of these is in a copse with birches, bracken and heather. When leaving, unless vehicle ground clearance is good, it would pay to exit

← Ben Hope towers above the more northerly of the two launch beaches.

↓ The gap carved by the Strathmore River as it approaches the head of the loch.

southwards and then turn at a convenient point if necessary as there is quite a drop from the tarmac.

The loch's name comes from the Norse hop, bay, to which the loch runs northwards. The loch is fed by the Strathmore River, which enters between a line of peaks over which Ben Hope towers, initially past an area of marsh

A838
R Hope
Hope
Lochside

Eriboll

An Lean-chàrn

L Hope

Strathmore R
Ben Hope

→ A wooded outcrop on the lower loch

↓ An Lean-chàrn on the western side of Loch Hope.

with occasional furze bushes at Eilean Mor. For those with stamina there are some challenging walking routes from the head of the loch. The old Moine Path traverses the lower flanks of Ben Hope to head north-east to the top end of the Kyle of Tongue. Another track crosses the river and leads north-west to Eriboll, passing over the lower part of 521m An Lean-chàrn.

The loch widens for a couple of kilometres, towards the end of which it reaches its maximum depth of more than 50m. A hut circle site on the east bank overlooks the narrowing, from where the loch continues to taper down. There are gravel banks and beaches at intervals with rowan trees adding colour in the autumn. Occasional outcrops of rock add scenic beauty on a more approachable scale than at the head of the loch.

A cottage at Arnaboll has cairns opposite. Beyond it, a chambered cairn and a hut circle are evidence of further habitation opposite Lochside.

The loch becomes the swift River Hope at Hope, where it is crossed by the A838 north coast road.

Hope is 6km from the proposed Space Hub Sutherland, from which it is hoped to make the first launch in 2022 and to be launching a dozen flights a year by 2030. These will be the only vertical launches from the British mainland and will be for small commercial payloads, hence not requiring to keep the public a minimum of 8km from the launch of the larger rockets, as at Cape Canaveral.

↑ The start of the River Hope at Hope.

DISTANCE_____
9km from Eilean Mor to Hope

OS 1:50,000 SHEET_____
9 Cape Wrath

ARSON AND CULPABLE HOMICIDE

LOCH NAVER

Now Henny was grey, the snow was a falling,
When Sellar the factor, one night came calling.
'Get out with you fast!', his men
*   were a yelling,*
'We're burning the cottage
*   of Henny Munroe'*
'We've orders from
*   Sutherland, Duke*
*   of this county,*
It's wanted for sheep so
*   away you must go!'*
The one of his company
*   threw in a faggot*
And frightened the life out of Henny Munroe!
JIM MCLEAN

Loch Naver runs north-east at the heart of the Flow Country, a huge blanket bog covering much of the area in the north of the Highlands. The River Vagastie and the River Mudale each feed into the head of the loch at Altnaharra. The B873 follows the north shore of the loch, giving little indication of the previous turbulent history of Strathnaver and its atrocities. These days there are only fir trees in forests and anglers in boats on the water. As with many other single-track roads

with passing places, there is a shortage of places to pull off the road near the water, although Grummore offers a possibility.

The south side of the upper loch is dominated by Ben Klibreck, rising up to 981m Meall nan Con, its height emphasized as aircraft on training flights pass well below its summit as they follow above the loch. Quieter fliers include redstarts and the inevitable midges.

There are hut circles on both sides of the loch at its upper end and standing

↓ Looking down the central part of the loch.

↓ The remains of the broch at Grummore. Across the loch is part of Ben Klibreck.

↑ Contorted rowan tree opposite Grumbeg.

stones below Ben Klibreck. The loch is at its deepest, some 30m, towards this end. A wooded island on the south side was used as a broch site during the Iron Age.

A heap of stones at the far end of the Altnaharra Caravan & Motorhome Club Campsite at Grummore is the remains of another broch, showing the hamlet to have been occupied for at least 2,000 years, until 1819. This is the first of a couple of dozen villages down Strathnaver that were subject to Clearances for the profits made from sheep rearing.

The arch culprit was Patrick Sellar, a factor, sheep farmer and lawyer who had managed to leave the court free in 1816 after facing charges of arson and culpable homicide. The case was presided over by Lord Pitmilly, whose bullying approach did much for Sellar's acquittal. Sellar admitted to a sadistic enjoyment of breaking people in court himself. Here, he had 16 houses torched

↓ The foot of the loch with isolated peaks to the east.

in 1819, their occupants evicted as part of his Clearance scheme where he made many thousands of people homeless to make way for sheep rearing. One resident further down Strathnaver, on a hilltop at night, counted 250 cottages in flames, some belonging to his friends. Of the occupants who survived, many emigrated.

Grumbeg's history goes back even further. A Neolithic chambered cairn is thought to be 4,400 to 6,000 years old. After a Clearance attack in 1814, there was a further visit in 1819. It was remembered for the story of Henny Munro, who had followed her husband, a soldier, on his campaigns until he died. She returned to Grumbeg, where neighbours assisted in providing her with basic furniture. When Sellar's men came to burn the five cottages, she pleaded and was allowed half an hour to get her furniture and

DISTANCE_____
9km from Altnaharra to the River Naver

OS 1:50,000 SHEET_____
16 Lairg & Loch Shin

valuables out. However, she was unable to get them far enough away from the building and the heat set fire to them so that she lost everything. The hillside, below 294m Pole Hill, is littered with stones and the remains of walls, the view over the length of the loch a monument to the atrocities perpetrated here and in many parts of northern Scotland in the name of profit.

The water begins to speed up past another broch site as it feeds into the River Naver.

↓ Sheep droppings and the remains of cottages at Grumbeg. Ben Klibreck stands above the head of the loch.

LOCH GARRY

SECLUDED BUT NOT REMOTE

43

Loch Garry is an impounded section of the River Garry. There is a road along nearly all of the north side, but most of it is single track with passing places and virtually nowhere to pull off. The nearest accessible launch point to the head of the loch is at a bridge across the loch, where there is limited parking at each end.

At its head the loch is joined by the Allt Lòn Glas Bheinn in an area of black silt behind what appear to be the remains of a training wall. The loch itself is clean, but the first 3km are shallow, often with weed growing up from the bed. The few users above the bridge are anglers in rowing boats.

The shoreline is nearly all wooded, some fragments of the ancient Caledonian pine forest and other conifers, larches, alders and birches, with some heather along the shore. There is a treeline, however, and the tops of hills are bare but for the windfarm that runs from

LOCH GARRY

← Ben Tee and other summits in Glengarry Forest.

Mullach Coire Ardachaidh towards 788m Meall Dubh.

Martins swoop around the bridge, but wildlife is limited. Greenfield Burn joins from the south and then the loch begins to deepen to a maximum of more than 50m. Salmon farming takes place in the shallows at the edge of the loch below Laddie Wood, reached by RIB.

The Allt Ladaidh drops down through the wood as the loch reaches towards a dark wooded cliff on the south shore.

↓ Sgùrr Chòinich and Glas Bheinn stand beyond the head of Loch Garry.

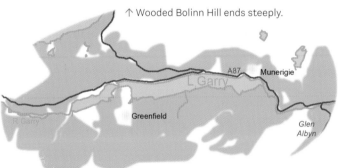

↑ Wooded Bolinn Hill ends steeply.

On the north side the road joins the A87 and access to the loch becomes easier as there are sections of old road next to the shore, giving places to park and short walks to the water.

The loch is at its most attractive beyond Bolinn Hill. Garbh Eilean and several other wooded islands are dotted about a widening of the loch.

A hydroelectric dam brings the loch to a halt 4km short of Loch Oich. The last place to take out is at Munerigie, where the wooded shoreline has bracken and healthy growths of moss but also midges. Care needs to be taken of the many fragments of glass on the stone beaches.

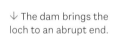

DISTANCE _____
11km from Garrygualach to the dam

OS 1:50,000 SHEET _____
34 Fort Augustus, Glen Roy & Glen Moriston

↓ The dam brings the loch to an abrupt end.

→ Wind turbines cover the hillside from Mullach Coire Ardachaidh.

LOCH NESS

HOME OF THE MONSTER

44

A visitor once to Loch Ness
Met the monster, who left him a mess;
They returned his entrails
By the regular mails
And the rest of the stuff by express.
ANON

LOCH NESS

Landing pontoons are adjacent to the entrance to Loch Ness. Loch Ness is Scotland's most famous loch. It is 36km long and covers 56 sq km. It contains the greatest volume of freshwater in Britain, is deeper than the North Sea at 250m and has the greatest mean depth of any British lake at 130m, 1.8m more than before the Caledonian Canal was constructed.

The shores are steep with underwater cliffs and the sea rises quickly with fierce squalls. Waves of 1.5m height are not unusual, sometimes they are twice as high. It therefore needs to be treated with great respect in bad weather, particularly when the wind is the prevailing south-westerly that blows straight down the loch. The wave action and steep bed and sides mean that wildlife is not as extensive as on the smaller lochs. However, the water is clearer and it has never been known to freeze, the temperature remaining fairly constant at 5–7°C, especially at the bottom. What it lacks in wildlife, it makes up for in scenery, particularly in fine weather. Some of the cloud effects can produce majestic or threatening skies. There is a *Loch Ness*

film and in 1970 it was used for filming part of *The Private Life of Sherlock Holmes*.

As the loch leaves Fort Augustus it is rejoined by the River Oich on the north side. The River Tarff flows in on the south side.

There is a crannog on Cherry Island, the only island in the loch, and Roman material has been found. There is also a Cherry Island Walk nature trail.

↓ A Loch Ness lighthouse at Fort Augustus. Sailing vessels from Norway and St Pierre & Miquelon at the head of the loch.

The tall trees at Allt na Criche were planted by Lord Lovat, the founder of the Forestry Commission. Opposite, the Allt Doe descends over a waterfall to enter the loch. A sheet of scree slides down Horseshoe Crag from 555m Beinn a' Bhacaidh, facing across to 607m high Burach. The latter is surrounded by Portclair Forest, covered with deciduous trees on its lower slopes, interwoven with bluebells in the spring. Portclair itself is the smallest of hamlets.

General Wade's bridge over the River Moriston was built after the 1715 Jacobite uprising. Opposite, the bed of Loch Ness reaches its steepest, dropping 199m in just 110m.

Above Alltsigh, tucked away in Creag-nan-Eun Forest, the glen sides reach their highest with Meall Fuar-mhonaidh rising to 699m.

Conspicuous on the east side is an

↑ Mountains rise steeply from Loch Ness near Invermoriston.

→ Urquhart Castle is one of Scotland's most visited castles, now and historically.

aerial before Foyers. A woodland walk is echoed by a forest trail at Inverfarigaig. First comes Easter Boleskine with its pre-1777 church and many burial enclosures. The Farigaig Forest trail has an interpretation centre in a converted stone stable, showing the development of the forest, and has a picnic area and public toilets. Near the River Farigaig there are the Inverfarigaig vitrified forts. There is another fort site on the west side of the loch. Goosanders might be seen on the loch, too.

The Cobb Memorial is dedicated to John Cobb, who was killed in 1952 while trying to set a new world water speed record on the loch in his jet speedboat, *Crusader*, which flipped and exploded.

An Iron Age Pictish vitrified fort at Strone Point in 580 was used as the site for the Grants' Urquhart Castle. At one time it was one

of the largest castles in Scotland, commanding the junction of Glen Urquhart with Glen Albyn. Mostly post-1509, it has additions by John Grant of Freuchie, who received it as a gift from James IV. It was sacked in 1689 and, in 1692, blown up by William of Orange's troops

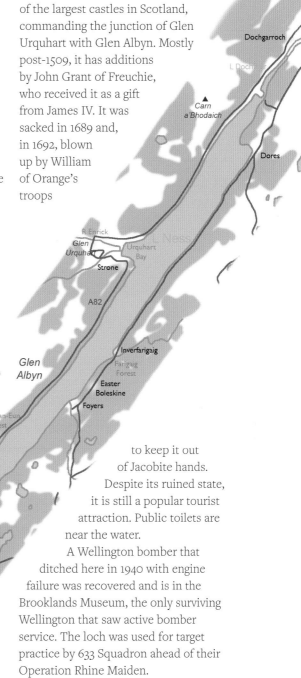

to keep it out of Jacobite hands. Despite its ruined state, it is still a popular tourist attraction. Public toilets are near the water.

A Wellington bomber that ditched here in 1940 with engine failure was recovered and is in the Brooklands Museum, the only surviving Wellington that saw active bomber service. The loch was used for target practice by 633 Squadron ahead of their Operation Rhine Maiden.

It is hard to think of Loch Ness

→ Not what you thought. Appearances can be deceiving. This was a bull orca with a flacid fin, seen off Alaska.

without also thinking of Nessie, the Loch Ness monster. Traditionally shown as a huge serpent with a series of coils looping out of the water, recent drawings suggest a more spherical body with a long neck and small head, perhaps also with four flippers. Recorded sightings go back to a kelpie seen by St Columba in 565. Saint Adamnan, monk of St Columba and Bishop of Iona, and the monks of Fort Augustus Abbey, the successors of St Columba, also recorded sightings.

Until 1935, General Wade's Military Road up the east side of the glen was the route through. The opening of the A82 brought tourists with many more sightings and photographs. The Japanese have even searched the depths of the loch with a mini submarine. As yet, conclusive proof has not been forthcoming.

Nessieland and the Loch Ness Centre & Exhibition in Drumnadrochit put the case for the monster. The findings of a 20-year scientific study said there are only 20–30 tonnes of fish in the loch, and they would not be able to support more than 2–3 tonnes of monster. The surface temperature only rises above 12°C for four months of the year, so the suggestion is that people are probably seeing an occasional cold water fish migrating in from the sea. The preferred option is the sturgeon. It can grow to more than 4m long and weigh in at 100kg.

Drumnadrochit lies between the River Coiltie and the River Enrick. Below is a swamp, where beaver were present until at least the 15th century.

Picnic sites line the east shore. The west shore has the Loch Ness Clansman Hotel with its own harbour. The dipper is present along the shoreline.

The west shore rises to 501m at scree-coated Carn a'Bhodaich, but the east side of the loch is lower. The width halves abruptly at Dores with a ridge bearing the Kinchyle of Dores stone circle and then Aldourie Castle, nearly at the end of the loch at Bona Ferry. Bona Lighthouse, the world's most advanced when built, was Britain's smallest manned inland lighthouse but now has holiday apartments.

DISTANCE

38km from Ft Augustus to Ballindarroch

OS 1:50,000 SHEETS

26 Inverness & Loch Ness
34 Fort Augustus, Glen Roy & Glen Moriston
(35 Kingussie & Monadhliath Mountains)

LOCH ERICHT

USED BY CLIMBERS AND FUGITIVES

LOCH ERICHT

Leaving the well-known bridge and pathway above to the forest,
Turning below from the track of the carts over stone and shingle,
Piercing a wood, and skirting a narrow and natural causeway
Under the rocky wall that hedges the bed of the streamlet,
Rounded a craggy point, and saw on a sudden before them
Slabs of rock, and a tiny beach, and perfection of water,
Picture-like beauty, seclusion sublime, and the godess of bathing.
ARTHUR HUGH CLOUGH

On the line of the Ericht-Laidon Fault and subsequently glaciated, Loch Ericht runs nearly straight, south-west directly into the prevailing headwind. This makes it something of a wind tunnel with rough water at times, perhaps with potential for setting surfing records along most of its 26km length.

Enlarged as part of the Tummel Hydro-Electric Power Scheme, increased in stages from 1928, it is 1km longer at each end than was its natural length. It has a surface area of 23 sq km and stores 230 million cubic metres of water, drawn from a 135 sq km catchment, mostly flowing directly into the loch. It has a dam at each end.

There is public road approach only at the Dalwhinnie end. Dalwhinnie is the highest village in the Highlands, at a junction of drovers' roads. From 1724, it was on the first military road from Drumochter, subsequently the A9, although the current line of the A9 is further from the village, which boasts its own distillery.

There is no vehicle public access past the station, but vehicles can be taken as far as the bridge under the Perth to Inverness railway where there is a locked barrier. Vehicles can be parked 200m from the southern end of Dalwhinnie Dam.

In the Grampians just outside the Cairngorms National Park, the loch is 351m above sea level, higher than the

↓ Ben Alder Lodge with Ben Alder beyond.

↑ The hill overlooking Alder Bay.

↓ Cottages at what was formerly the head of the loch.

which passes underneath the dam.

The former head of the loch was by the cottages at the end of the initial area of forest on the south-east side of the loch. Much more forest is on the opposite side where the dense Loch Ericht Forest follows for 13km at the foot of the Fara, a 10km-long ridge up to 911m high.

Red deer may be present on this side and there may be ospreys and eagles. The shoreline is mostly gravel or small rocks.

On the south-east side the land rises to 772m Creagan Mór and 917m Geal Chàrn, a Munro. Across the loch is Ben Alder Lodge, pink with turrets. Behind the lodge the peaks of Ben Alder Forest rise steadily to Ben Alder, another Munro at 1,148m. This is one of the greatest wildernesses in Scotland.

Beinn Udlamain, a peak of Dalnaspidal

village. The 4.5m high dam of 1937, 350m long, is more of a wave wall to protect the village and to prevent water being lost to the River Truim. On the other hand, the Cuaich Aqueduct brings water from Loch Cuaich and feeds it through a culvert,

← The Cuaich Aqueduct discharges into Loch Ericht, a convenient launching point.

Truim

Cuaich
Aqueduct

Dalwhinnie

▲
The
Fara

A9

▲
Creagan
Mór

L Ericht
Forest

▲
Geal-charn

Ben
Alder
Forest

Dalnaspidal
Forest

▲
Beinn
Udlamain

L Ericht

▲
Ben
Alder

▲
Stob an
Aonich Mhóir

Talla Bheith
Forest

Rannoch
Forest

↓ The power station fed from Loch Garry.

▲
Srôn
Bheag

R Ericht

Forest, dominates the south-east side before a small power station is reached. Built in 1962, this generates 2.2MW from water fed at a 55m head from Loch Garry. There are also some cottages here at the start of a long private road to Loch Rannoch.

Talla Bheith Forest drops steeply from 855m Stob an Aonaich Mhòir with a conspicuous area of gorse and birches down near the loch.

The Alder Burn feeds into Alder Bay on the north-west side beyond an unusual hill in the shape of a truncated cone. Cluny's Cage, named after Cluny MacPherson, was here, a hidden cave obscured by trees, used by Prince Charlie after his defeat at Culloden.

Some hill walkers choose to approach Ben Alder by kayak, landing at Ben Alder Cottage, to reduce the length of the trek in.

The land becomes lower on the west side, at least as far back as Rannoch Forest. A spur on the west side, fed by the Cam Chriochan, was the original

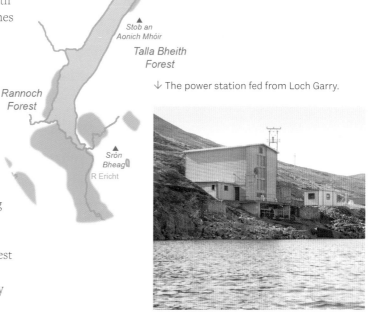

↑ The dry River Ericht crosses moorland below the Ericht Dam.

↓ The River Ericht's water crosses its watercourse.

foot of the loch. The extended loch now curves around to the south-east as the shore becomes increasingly of soft sand studded with boulders and tree stumps.

Ahead is the 340m long Ericht Dam, 14m high, failure of which would cause a domino effect of failures of other dams downstream. The River Ericht is now virtually dry as its water goes into a large pipeline that feeds it directly to the power station on Loch Rannoch.

Take out is easier at the south-west end of the dam and then across the dam. A 5km road, the tarmac starting to break up in places but generally sound, leads across moorland, past bracken and fir plantations to Bridge of Ericht near the head of Loch Rannoch. The road ends at locked gates, but there is a pedestrian gate tucked away in the corner, which is not locked.

DISTANCE_____
26km from Dalwhinnie to the Ericht Dam

OS 1:50,000 SHEET_____
42 Glen Garry & Loch Rannoch

LOCH RANNOCH

THE LONGEST OPEN WATER ON ONE OF SCOTLAND'S LONGEST INLAND ROUTES

46

Such are the scenes, where savage grandeur wakes
An awful thrill that softens into sighs;
Such feelings rouse them by dim Rannoch's lakes.
SIR WALTER SCOTT

LOCH RANNOCH

The most distant of the River Tummel's headwaters is the River Bà, which emerges from Bealach Fuar-chathaidh on the flanks of Clach Leathad. Eventually it joins the River Tay to give one of Scotland's longest inland routes.

It is as the River Gaur that the route meets Loch Rannoch, the longest stretch of open water on the route. The River Ericht joins unobtrusively at Bridge of Ericht. It used to bring in water from Loch Ericht and water piped from Loch Garry, but now most of its water is sent by pipeline. It is delivered by penstocks leading down the hillside to the obvious 1930 Rannoch Power Station by the loch. The 156m head of water gives it a 44MW capacity and it produces the most power

↓ The west end of Loch Rannoch, looking towards Glen Coe.

↑ The crannog and oystercatchers with the Rannoch Power Station beyond.

of any of the nine power stations in the Tummel hydroelectricity scheme with all its dams, weirs and pipelines.

In the centre of the loch on Eilean nan Faoileag is the strange little tower of a crannog, while the southern shore is dominated by one of the largest oak woods remaining in Scotland, part of

Rannoch Forest and the Tay Forest Park. Red squirrels are numerous around the loch. In the more typical fir part at Carie a set of walks is laid out for the public. On the northern shore, opposite these, is the site of Clach na h'Jobairte.

The northern shore at Kinloch Rannoch is overlooked by a number

→ The view down the loch from the crannog.

of modern holiday flats. If the wind is from the west the surf increases steadily towards the eastern end of the loch and waves may begin to break before the end is reached.

The south-east corner of the loch has a memorial near a viewpoint and a settlement site.

As the water leaves the loch it becomes the River Tummel.

DISTANCE_____
 15km from Bridge of Gaur to Kinloch Rannoch

OS 1:50,000 SHEETS_____
 42 Glen Garry & Loch Rannoch
 (51 Loch Tay & Glen Dochart)

↑ The south shore at the eastern end of the loch.

↓ Schiehallion rises beyond the east end of the loch.

47

LOCH TUMMEL

THE VIEW THAT MADE SCOTLAND FASHIONABLE

LOCH TUMMEL

Sure by Tummel and Loch Rannoch and Lochaber I will go
By heather tracks wi' heaven in their wiles.
If it's thinkin' in your inner heart the braggart's in my step,
You've never smelled the tangle o' the Isles.
KENNETH MACLEOD

As well as being shorter than Loch Rannoch, Loch Tummel is protected by islands at its east end, narrowing down and bending away from the wind.

Errochty Power Station of 1957 at the head of the loch collects water from the River Bruar, the River Garry and Loch Errochty, its 186m head giving it a capacity of 75MW, the largest in the Tummel hydroelectric power scheme. However, its

→ Frenich Wood and Sron Mhòr from Bohally.

↓ Looking up the loch from Queen's View.

annual power output is exceeded by the Rannoch, Tummel Bridge (on the river above the loch) and Clunie power stations. Its facing is of stone excavated from the tunnel.

There is a small private jetty on the south side of the loch, 2km from its head at Donlellan.

Tummel Forest stands to the north and Tay Forest Park stretches away to the south with a homestead site in Frenich Wood and more on the north shore of the loch opposite Mains of Duntanlich.

More importantly, though, the loch was popular with Queen Victoria. It was her love of the Highlands that made Scotland fashionable and started the tourist trade. The viewpoint at Queen's View registers that this was her favourite spot after visiting in 1866. It looks up Loch Tummel towards the peak of Schiehallion. However, the name probably comes from Robert the Bruce's Queen Isabella. There are walks laid out in Allean Forest.

↑ The private jetty near the head of Loch Tummel.

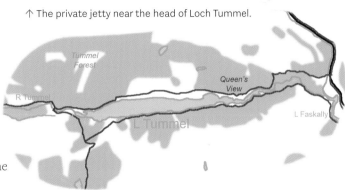

The loch is retained by Clunie Dam, which pipes the water to Clunie Power Station on the artificial Loch Faskally. Again, the River Tummel is left with only compensation water.

DISTANCE
11km (from Dalcroy to Clunie Dam

OS 1:50,000 SHEETS
(42 Glen Garry & Loch Rannoch)
43 Braemar & Blair Atholl
52 Pitlochry & Crieff

48

LOCH TAY

LOCH LIVING TO A FAULT

LOCH TAY

When I've done my work of day,
And I row my boat away,
Doon the waters of Loch Tay,
As the evening light is fading
And I look upon Ben Lawers
Where the after glory glows;
And I think on two bright eyes
And the melting mouth below.
BOULTON & MACLEOD

Two rivers meet in a delta at the head of Loch Tay at Killin. The River Dochart arrives after descending the Falls of Dochart, unusual for scenic falls in not being narrow and high. The River Lochay is placid, with cruisers moored by the Killin Hotel, where there is a gated slipway (and mallards used to getting food).

The railway bridge over the river remains in place, despite the line closure in 1965. The route led north to Finlarig Castle, built in 1609 by the Campbells of Glenorchy. One of the castle's features used to be a beheading pit complete with the Maiden, a crude guillotine. Adjacent is Killin Golf Club.

Alders give way to more open land where the trees tend to be dead skeletons grounded on the bed of the river. Reeds appear and there are swans. A boathouse stands on the bank just before the combined rivers open out into the loch.

The glacial Loch Tay, up to 1.7km wide, runs north-east, its fertile banks on limestone. The Killin end receives 500mm more rain per year than the Kenmore end. The A827 follows the north-west shore. A minor road, the Rob Roy Way, follows the southeast side. There is little parking on either side, even when the roads do come near the water. Salmon are present in the peaty water.

↓ The Falls of Dochart in Killin.

← Placid moorings on the River Lochay.

↓ Edinburgh University's Firbush Point Field Centre.

A penstock runs conspicuously down the mountainside from Lochan na Lairige to a power station on the north bank of the loch. A Munro, Meall nan Tarmachan is 1,043m high.

Edinburgh University's Firbush Point Field Centre is on the south bank. A break in the trees on top of the ridge behind is the site of a fort, the mountainside dipping to the Allt Breaclaich before rising again to the summit of 637m Creag Gharbh.

The Allt a' Mhoirneas and Burn of Edramucky flow down to the north shore past the Morenish memorial chapel of 1902 in Arts & Crafts style. Milton Morenish has Loch Tay Marina. A range of watersports take place on the loch, including water skiing.

The shore is wooded on the north side for several kilometres and birds might range from Canada geese to ospreys.

Ardeonaig, on the south shore, has red squirrels. The Ardeonaig Burn passes the site of Cill mo Chormaig, the pre Reformation church with St Cormac's cell, and the remains of the 16th century Mains Castle. Above the shore is a felsite sill.

↓ Sròn a Chlachain at the head of the loch, leading back towards Sgiath Chùil.

↑ A replica crannog at Kenmore.

→ Ben Lawers, head in the clouds, is the tenth highest of Scotland's mountains.

↓ The Loch Tay Fault runs away to the left of Fearnan.

The 80km-long Loch Tay Fault, running from Loch Lubnaig to Glen Tilt, passes through Ardeonaig and Fearnan, the section of loch that turns in a more northerly direction. The fault's lateral displacement is some 7km.

Facing is 1,214m Ben Lawers, the largest massif in the southern Highlands, from the summit of which the Atlantic and the North Sea may be seen on a clear day. Of highly calcareous schist, it is the best area in Britain for alpine plants, some unique in Britain to this site. Wild flowers include alpine forget-me-nots and gentians, purple and yellow saxifrage and montane scrub.

The north-west shore becomes more open and agricultural. The Lawers Burn enters the loch by a roofless church.

The stone circle at Machuim may have been a double circle until the outer one was removed to make more land available for agriculture.

Facing, the Allt a' Chilleine passes through Ardtalnaig where there is more

↑ Beinn Bhreac covered with heather.

felsite above the shore. Below 716m Beinn Bhreac the loch's depth is more than 150m, the bed 46m below sea level.

A boathouse is conspicuous on the east shore, while a cross is hidden in the woods on the west side.

The Acharn Burn descends over the scenic Falls of Acharn by a cave and flows out into the loch at Acharn Point. Along the hillside are a series of antiquities, stone and hut circles, tumulus, cup and ring-marked rocks and more beyond the end of the loch. The loch becomes increasingly busy with boats from sailing vessels to jet skis, partly as a result of the Croft-na-Caber watersports centre and Taymouth Marina on the south shore.

There are at least 18 Iron Age crannog sites around the loch, but a new one has been built here. The Scottish Crannog Centre is to move to a bigger site on the north shore where a collection of perhaps three crannogs will be built, which should reduce the pressure here where parking is very restricted.

Drummond Hill, on the north side, has a substantial dark forest of fir trees with forest walks, overlooking an island with a castle site. The conspicuous structure at Kenmore, at the end of the loch, is the segmented arch bridge of 1774. Of local chlorite schist and slate, it has ornamentation while large oculi save weight. The River Tay departs under the bridge and through glacial deposits, under the eye of 567m Craig Hill.

The village's beach, lawn surround and accessible parking are beside the A827 on the south side of the loch, with a variety of activity by, on and in the water on a summer's day.

DISTANCE
24km from Killin to Kenmore

OS 1:50,000 SHEETS
51 Loch Tay
(52 Pitlochry & Aberfeldy)

LOCH EARN

WATERSPORTS IN THE SOUTHERN HIGHLANDS

LOCH EARN

But, for the place-say, couldst though learn
Nought of the friendly clans of Earn?
SIR WALTER SCOTT

→ The 1790 version of Ardvorlich House overlooks Loch Earn.

↓ Loch Earn looking from Lochearnhead towards St Fillans.

There is a convenient parking spot by a watersports centre at Lochearnhead, complete with public toilets. The first few hundred metres can be hazardous owing to the activities of water skiers, but they are soon left behind. A crannog site stands just off the south shore at Edinample.

An unsuccessful fish farm on the north bank suffered sabotage attempts in 1982, allegedly by anglers. This led to 30,000 trout being released into Loch Earn for anglers to catch.

The loch is surrounded by mountains with trees along the shoreline and heather above. After some 4km, 985m Ben Vorlich, hill of the bay, appears from behind 740m Ben Our on the south side, a solid block of mountain, aloof and

remote from the relative foothills.

Ardvorlich House, which was visited by Sir Walter Scott, was Darnlinvarach Castle, the meeting place for the clans, in his historical novel *A Legend of Montrose*. It was actually the principal Stewart household. A group of MacGregors visited the castle in the 17th century

and were given the customary hospitality. However, as people who were not friends, they were given the cold shoulder and served cold meat rather than a hot meal. While the pregnant Lady Margaret Stewart was out of the room, they placed on a silver plate the head of her brother, John Drummond, whom they had previously murdered, with cold meat stuffed into his mouth. She ran up the glen to Beinn Domhnaill, where she gave birth to James Stewart, who was to play a major part in the Covenanting Wars, despite his periods of madness, and appears in Scott's novel as Allan M'Aulay.

Arrival at the east end of the loch is foreshadowed by the Loch Earn Leisure Park caravan site on the south bank and by moorings and the presence of dinghies, yachts and windsurfers.

The River Earn leads from the loch at St Fillans, a quiet narrow channel of clear peat brown water.

To the south-east of the village is the site of Dundurn fort, the name perhaps from its appearance from the north of an upturned clenched fist. It is considered the finest nuclear fort known. The central

boss is approached through a series of walled courts, each overlooked by the one above. It was besieged in 683 and King Giric died here in c890. In the 6th century it had been used as St Fillan's Chair and was said to be used to cure back rheumatism. His seat is comfortable, but the full cure required the patient to be pulled down the hill afterwards on his back by his feet. St Fillan's Well was said to have been effective for treating ailments in August, even when it moved itself here from the top of Dunfillan Hill.

DISTANCE
10km from Lochearnhead to St Fillans

OS 1:50,000 SHEET
51 Loch Tay & Glen Dochart

← St Fillans has a sculpture trail.

↓ An island in the loch at St Fillans.

50 LOCH KATRINE

DIRTY DEALINGS BY THE CLEANEST WATER

LOCH KATRINE

*Loch Katrine lay beneath him roll'd,
In all her length far winding lay,
With promontory, creek, and bay,
And islands that, empurpled bright,
Floated amid a livelier light,
And mountains, that like giants stand,
To sentinel enchanted land.*

SIR WALTER SCOTT

Because the loch was used to supply water to Glasgow since 1859 boats were banned from it, with the exception of the SS *Sir Walter Scott* from 1900 onwards. However, that changed with the Land Reform (Scotland) Act of 2003 and small unpowered craft are now welcome.

Stronachlacher is the preferred launch point as it is less crowded,

the parking is free and it is visited less by the SS *Sir Walter Scott*, which approaches quietly and is difficult to manoeuvre, especially in the confined space at the south-east end of the loch. The Pier Café at Stronachlacher is available for refreshments and there are public toilets. Launching is at the far end of the lawn from the pier, down a bank, over a stream and onto a stony beach.

Serious public interest in Loch Katrine began in 1817 with publication of Sir Walter Scott's *Rob Roy*, after which visitors flocked to the loch. Scott also used the loch as inspiration for *The Lady of the Lake*.

The loch is all in the Loch Lomond & the Trossachs National Park, in Stirling,

↓ The SS *Sir Walter Scott* returns to base.

↑ The pier and café at Stronachlacher.

and runs south-east through Strath
Gartney. There are some interesting
folding and sides that can be rocky and
precipitous in places.

   The first part of the loch is held back
by what resembles a causeway with a gap
in it, resulting in silt being deposited on
each side of the channel, but the water is
clear thereafter. Waders, herons, Canada
geese, shelducks and oystercatchers may

↑ Meall Mór above
the head of the loch.

▲
Beinn
a' Choin

Strath Gartney

Stronachlachar

L Katrine

L Arklet

The
Trossachs

Ben ▲
Venue

Achray

← Rocky shoreline
at Coilachra with
An Garadh beyond.

↓ Black Island sits below An Garadh.

→ Cattle on the shore below Meall Dearg.

↑ Folding on rocks forming the shoreline.

↓ Cruinn Bheinn, An Stuichd and Meall Gaothach.

be seen and the cuckoo heard. Birches, conifers, oaks, rowans and heather add colour. There are shingle beaches to be found in places.

Glengyle House is prominent with the Sput Dubh waterfall above it and the Clan Gregor graveyard nearby. Rob Roy was born here. The peaks rise to 865m Stob a'Choin to the north and 770m Beinn a' Choin to the west.

A boathouse stands beside the loch.

Portnellan has more Clan Gregor graves. The tree-covered Black Island is where Rob Roy held the factor of the Duke of Montrose captive for three days.

Loch Katrine is deeper from here, Loch Arklet, at the foot of 598m Beinn Uamha, having been deepened with the installation of a dam.

Royal Cottage is the draw-off point for the 42km gravity pipeline to Glasgow. It is some of the best water in Britain, its

softness being so effective at removing dirt that soap sales in Glasgow halved. Successive dams have increased the level in the loch by 4.3m.

Cattle stand in the water so it is not quite pristine. Huge clumps of peat moss are found in the woods below 727m Ben Venue and opposite 696m Taobh na Coille. There is another boathouse on the north shore.

Boaters wishing to visit the Trossachs Pier Complex are advised that it is far easier and safer to land in the bay to the south-east of Eilean Molach, Ellen's Isle, and walk along the cycle track that skirts the north side of the loch. The general advice is to keep to the sides of the loch, well clear of the passage of the SS *Sir Walter Scott*.

Corrie na Urisgean, the Goblin's Cave, is where the eastern end of the loch becomes steeper and more closed in. The Trossachs, the bristled territory,

begin here as the loch becomes Achray Water to reach a set of sluices.

↑ Looking down the loch towards Meall Gainmheich.

DISTANCE——————————
13km from Glengyle to Trossachs Pier

OS 1:50,000 SHEETS——————
56 Loch Lomond & Inveraray
57 Stirling & the Trossachs

INDEX